St. Andrew's By-The-Sea

The Outer Banks COMPANION

D1609639

In the Episcopal Diocese of East Carolina

ISBN 0-9705884-0-2

Printed in the USA by

WIMMER
The Wimmer Companies
Memphis
1-800-548-2537

INTRODUCTION BY JAN KARON,
AUTHOR OF THE MITFORD SERIES

Dear Friends and Fellow Cooks,

Because of the attention to food in the Mitford books, people often say, "I bet you're a great cook!"

I'm not a great cook. My sister, Brenda, is a great cook. My mother, Wanda, is a great cook. I'm merely a good cook. In truth, I'm rather timid as a cook, unlike a friend who once described herself as "fearless in the kitchen." Also, I'm impatient. I want to be writing, not cooking.

Happily, I've found a way to do both at the same time.

When working at my desk, I love to have a chicken roasting in the oven. Rubbed with oil and fresh garlic, and stuffed with half a lemon and a sprig of rosemary, this may be the most heavenly aroma (and prod to creativity) on earth.

I'm also made happier in my labors by a pot of beans simmering on the stove. First, I sauté onions in my Dutch oven 'til golden, then add water and soaked beans, coarse salt, lots of thyme, a splash of olive oil and whatever else lures me to the spice shelf.

In truth, we sometimes fail to be lured at all by what's on hand. Which is where the wisdom of doing something with nothing comes in.

"Oddly," says cookbook author, Susan Wiegand, "it is not real cooks who insist that the finest ingredients are necessary to produce a delicious something... Real cooks take stale bread and aging onions and make you happy."

Whatever the fare, my family always enjoys asking a blessing — in crowded restaurants, on a picnic, or at home. This gesture of remembrance to our Lord for His graciousness always makes us feel better — happier, somehow. It reminds us yet again that, in the words of the little child's blessing, God is great, God is good.

Oh, and for heaven's sake, do remember in your blessing the cook and his or her contribution to the table! As Louella once said after a blessing by Father Tim, "You didn' say nothin' to th' Lord 'bout my beans!"

I hope you'll look for the Mitford cookbook in the not-too-distant future. It will contain recipes for all the more intriguing dishes mentioned in the Mitford novels, including Percy Mosely's Incomplete Guide to Grill Cooking, Esther Bolick's famous Orange Marmalade Cake, Edith Mallory's seductive Crab Cobbler, and even the lowly Rector's Meatloaf (you probably don't want to make this).

And so, my friends at St. Andrew's By-the-Sea, I pray on this golden, nearly-spring morning in the mountains that His peace be in your hearts, His provisions upon your tables, and His tender care and mercy upon your home and loved ones, always.

Your friend, Jan Karon

The Cookbook Project

The Cookbook Committee worked for nearly two years gathering recipes, researching history and working with local artists to create this beautiful cookbook edition. It was a true labor of love and is a tribute to our wonderful church by the sea and all the people who contributed to making The Outer Banks Companion *a reality.*

ARTIST'S RENDITION OF PIPE ORGAN

Proceeds from the sale of this St. Andrew's By-the Sea Cookbook will be used for refurbishment of the organ donated by St. Paul's Episcopal Church, Edenton, NC.

Contributing Artists

The Outer Banks and St. Andrew's By-the-Sea are blessed to have many gifted individuals who express their talents through art. We are very fortunate to have these individuals contribute their artwork to *The Outer Banks Companion*.

Sandy Ball

Marcia Cline

Cecelia Anne Hill

Ann Hines

Ray Matthews

Wil Payne

Kerry Oaksmith-Sanders

John Silver

Peggy Stovall

Jean Winslow

The Youth of St. Andrew's

Cookbook Committee

Phyllis Bruce and Carol Brassington — *Co-chairs*

Lois Bradshaw and Virginia Overman — *Historians*

Elizabeth Davenport — *Fundraising*

Kathy Nolin and Louise Dollard — *Recipes*

Kerry Oaksmith-Sanders and Nancy Harvey — *Graphic Designers*

Special Acknowledgments

Elis Olsson Memorial Foundation

Marcia Cline — *Cover Art*

Jan DeBlieu, *Author* — *Excerpts from* Hatteras Journal *and* Wind

Ray Matthews — *Photography*

Jean Winslow — *Pen and Ink Sketches*

Outer Banks History Center — *Historical Archives and Photographs of St. Andrew's By-the-Sea*

Our History

Taken August 6. 1916
after the Consecration of St Andrews by th-Sea.

On August 18, 1850, the anniversary of the birth of Virginia Dare, the Rt. Rev. Silliman Ives consecrated All Saints, a sound side chapel in Nags Head, North Carolina, built for the use of the congregations of Edenton and Elizabeth City residents summering on the Outer Banks. In 1865, the chapel was torn down by order of General Burnside of the Federal Army to provide shelters for runaway slaves who had found refuge on Roanoke Island.

Under the leadership of the Rev. Robert Brent Drane, D. D., the compensation of $700 paid by the United States Congress for the loss of All Saints was used to construct a new church, consecrated on August 6, 1916 by the Rt. Rev. Thomas C. Darst, D. D. Mr. S. J. Twine, the builder of this new church named St. Andrew's By-the-Sea, also constructed many of the historic beachfront cottages in Nags Head. In 1937, St. Andrew's By-the-Sea was moved to its current location on the then newly built Virginia Dare Trail on the ocean side. The bell from the original All Saints, having been saved, was installed in a new belfry.

With the increase of permanent residents in Dare County, St. Andrew's attained Mission Status in 1955 and in 1968 came to full Parish Status. A Parish Hall was built in 1962. In the 1980's a wing to accommodate church schoolrooms and limited administration was added. The Nave of St. Andrew's By-the-Sea was consecrated on August 18, 1996, by the Rt. Rev. B. Sidney Sanders as part of the celebration of the 80th anniversary of the present edifice and its service to the Outer Banks. The continued growth of the congregation has lead to plans for the addition of much needed classroom and office spaces and a new Sanctuary. The beautiful American Gothic church that is St. Andrew's By-the-Sea will continue to serve all who love the Outer Banks.

This information and the visual materials have been derived
from church records and its printed materials, and from
the Outer Banks History Center, Manteo, North Carolina.

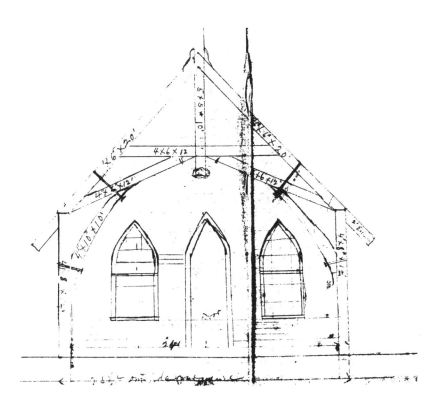

When Steven J. Twine arrived on the Outer Banks from Elizabeth City on the steamer, New Bern, in 1897, there was "not much to Nags Head."

He began to build cottages on the sound side in about 1909 and, in 1910, he built a cottage on the ocean front.

In 1917, Mr. Twine built St. Andrew's By-the-Sea on the sound side and his sketch of the framing of this wonderful example of American Gothic mirrors many of the cottages he built over the years on the ocean front.

St. Andrew's was moved to its present location in 1937 as more visitors chose to spend their summers close to the ocean.

For his work on the beautiful little chapel, Mr. Twine received the "grand sum" of $300.

source: Earl Dean – 1955

Rector's Preface:
The Outer Banks Companion

The kitchen is the place where banquets begin. The kitchen at Saint Andrew's By-the-Sea is such a place. Here, the family of Christ gathers around a large, central counter space and prepares food honoring significant events of our lives together. We feast at baptisms, confirmations, retirements, graduations, covered dish meals, and receptions honoring the Communion of Saints. Sometimes we feed the poor and those who otherwise would be eating alone. Always, we are seeking the companionship of Christ who took bread, blessed it, broke it, and distributed it; the Bread of Life.

Whether alone or in the company of friends, preparing a meal whets the appetite for companionship. Breaking bread together (com = with; panion = bread; ship = vessel) brings people into a common fellowship where stories of meaning can be shared as we are fed. It is a most satisfying experience. We pray, "give us this day our daily bread," knowing that the provision for every day of life is from the bounty and mercy of God.

Gather with us around the Holy Table and give thanks to God! And as you go forth from this place may this book offer you a taste of the hospitality of our Lord, Jesus Christ. From our kitchen by the sea where the smell of salt air blends with fresh baked aromas, we prepare but a sweet foretaste; let the heavenly Banquet begin with such memories.

Your Outer Banks Companions,
Saint Andrew's By-the-Sea,
The Rev. Charles E. B. Gill,
Rector

Table of Contents

Our present beautiful little church by the sea has provided a wonderful place for local residents and summer visitors to worship for 84 years. Neither the bitter storms nor the encroaching seas have prevented it from opening its doors to welcome all those who come to worship. In 1916, 50 worshipers built the church to accommodate 150. They obviously had a realistic vision of the future. The worshipers in 1999 were also faced with the challenge of providing for the growth of our church family well into the 21st century.

Appetizers

Appetizers, Soups, and Beverages

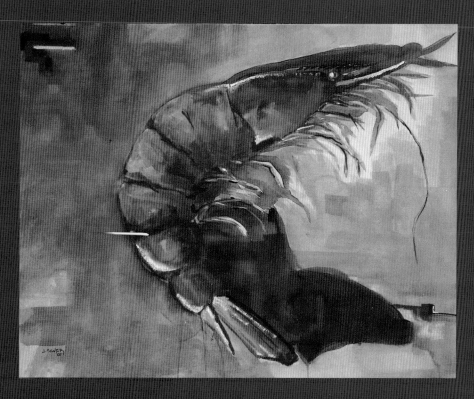

John Silver

Standing Knee-Deep in a Stream and Dying of Thirst

"Christians are like tea bags. You don't know how strong they are until they get in hot water."

The revelation that we have everything we need in life to make us happy, but simply lack the awareness to appreciate it can be as refreshing as a cold glass of iced tea on a hot summer afternoon. Or, it can be as shocking as having cold water thrown in our face. Many of us go through life parched and empty, thirsting after happiness, when we are really standing knee-deep in a stream of abundance. Life will get our attention one way or the other—with a sip or a splash. We can choose to quench our thirst for "the good life" by acknowledging the good that exists in our own lives. When we do this, we can then offer to others the gift of our grateful hearts.

Tipsy or Drunken Shrimp

2 pounds shrimp	½ teaspoon white pepper
¼ cup vegetable oil	2 tablespoons lemon juice
2 teaspoons salt	¼ cup dry vermouth

Peel shrimp and devein leaving tail section on. Add oil to an electric fry pan and heat oil to 320 degrees. Add shrimp, salt and pepper. Cook shrimp while frequently stirring for 8 to 10 minutes or until pink and tender. Increase electric fry pan heat to 420 degrees, add lemon juice and vermouth. Cook 1 minute and then scoop shrimp from pan and drain. Serve cold or hot as an appetizer with cocktail sauce or a light lemon sauce.

May also be served as a main dish for 2 to 3 servings.

Yield: 6 servings

Cheesy Shrimp

1 pound shrimp	2 tablespoons mayonnaise
2 ounces (½ stick) butter	1 teaspoon garlic salt
1 (5 ounce) jar Old English cheese	½ teaspoon seasoned salt
	8 English muffins

Boil shrimp, peel, devein, and chop fine. Blend butter, cheese, mayonnaise and salts and mix with shrimp. Split English muffins in half and then spread each half with shrimp mixture. Cut muffin halves into 4 wedges. Toast until light brown, a few at a time, in a small toaster oven.

The wedges may be frozen until needed; thaw and then toast them.

Try part shrimp and part crabmeat.

Yield: 64 wedges

"A different system of time operates on the [Outer Banks]. I call it island time. It is a way of life in which you learn not to make very firm plans, because at any moment something unexpected — a storm, a shift of wind, a blackout... may force you to change them. Few people care to know the exact time; it is enough to know the time within ten to fifteen minutes. Island people do not guard their hours as jealously as city people...

"Every day some work will get done and some will be left for tomorrow. You cannot force life to unfold at a faster pace; you will drive yourself crazy if you try. This relaxed philosophy is not from laziness or lack of character but from knowing that the island world can change at any moment, and not always for the better."

From Hatteras Journal *by Jan DeBlieu, 1987.*

Fantastic Shrimp Wheels

½ cup cooked
    shrimp,
    chopped fine
¼ cup mayonnaise
2 tablespoons
    green olives,
    chopped

2 tablespoons chili sauce
1 tablespoon celery,
    chopped fine
2 (8 ounce) packages
    crescent rolls

Combine all ingredients except crescent rolls in a bowl. Unroll crescent rolls and make 8 rectangles. Spread each rectangle with ¼ cup of the mixture. Roll up and cut each roll into 7 slices. Place on greased cookie sheet and bake at 325 degrees for 10 to 12 minutes.

Yield: 4½ dozen

Phyllis' Crabmeat Dip

6 ounces lump crabmeat
½ cup cheddar cheese,
    grated
4 tablespoons French
    dressing

1 teaspoon horseradish
    lemon juice, dash
    dill, onion or chives,
    optional, to taste

Mix all ingredients and chill before serving on crackers or party bread.

Yield: 4 to 6 servings

Hot or Cold Crabmeat Dip

24 ounces cream cheese, softened	½ teaspoon onion juice
½ cup mayonnaise	2 cloves garlic, pressed (or equivalent garlic powder)
¼ cup dry white wine	
2 tablespoons Dijon mustard	1 pound back fin crabmeat
1½ teaspoons powdered sugar	¼ cup fresh parsley, minced

Combine first seven ingredients and mix well. Fold crabmeat in gently. Heat in a double boiler or microwave until warmed through. Transfer to chafing dish or serve in warm microwave dish or may chill before serving with crackers. Sprinkle with parsley before serving.

May be frozen, thawed and rewarmed.

Yield: 25 to 30 servings

Prayer is for the soul, what food is for the body. The blessing of one prayer lasts until the next, just as the strength gained from one meal lasts 'til the one after.

Jewish Prayer.

Clams Coinjock

fresh clams	bacon chopped into 1 inch squares
Parmesan cheese, grated	Worcestershire sauce

Place as many clams as desired into freezer for 30 minutes to make them easier to open. Open and leave clams in one half the shell, discarding other half of shell. Sprinkle each clam liberally with grated Parmesan cheese and place squares of bacon over cheese. Cover each with Worcestershire sauce and grill or broil until bacon is crisp.

Yield: as many as you care to make

Smoked Tuna Pâté

6	fresh tuna steaks, about 1 inch thick	1	teaspoon seasoned salt
1	teaspoon lemon pepper	1	tablespoon mayonnaise
2	tablespoons sour cream	½	lemon, juice of
1	tablespoon Dijon mustard		salt and pepper, to taste
1	medium onion	3-4	sprigs parsley
1	teaspoon dill weed		paprika

Some early land grants in the Outer Banks: 1663 Carlyle Island to Sir John Colleton, now known as Colington; 1711 grant of 502 acres near Cape Hatteras and 480 acres at Keneckid Inlet, now known as Kinnakeet, to William Reed; 1713 present-day Core Banks and Shackleford Banks to John Porter; about 1719 Ocracoke Island to John Lovick; 1722 Bodie Island to Matthew Midget.

Various Sources.

Smoke tuna steaks for 2 to 2½ hours under low heat using hickory chips to enhance flavor. While this is being done, prepare remaining ingredients in a blender. When the tuna is ready, add chunks of cooked tuna to the blender. Entire batch should be blended to form a thick pâté (should only take about 2 to 3 minutes). Add water if necessary for desired consistency. Place in serving bowl and garnish with parsley and paprika.

Very, very nice when accompanied with a good white wine.

Add 1 diced jalapeño pepper if you like spicy food like contributing cook Ashby Baum.

Yield: 8 to 10 servings

Sister's Deviled Ham Spread

1	(8 ounce) package cream cheese	1½	teaspoons onions, minced
¼	cup (or less) green olives, pitted	⅓	cup bleu cheese dressing
1	(6½ ounce) can deviled ham (or two 4½ ounce cans)	½	cup mayonnaise

Mix and serve with crackers. If using two small cans of deviled ham instead of one large can, may increase mayonnaise to reach desired moisture and consistency.

Yield: 4 cups

Salmon Ball Spread

1 (8 ounce) package cream cheese, softened	¾ teaspoon garlic powder
1 tablespoon lemon juice	1 tablespoon mayonnaise
2 tablespoons onion, grated	1 teaspoon Greek seasoning
1 teaspoon Worcestershire sauce	16 ounces salmon, canned or fresh
1 teaspoon dill weed	fresh parsley, chopped

Blend all ingredients except salmon and parsley. Remove and discard dry skin and bones from salmon, and crumble salmon meat. Add to mixture and blend well. May adjust seasonings to taste. Form mixture into a ball or spoon into a fish mold. Cover with chopped parsley. Refrigerate 4 to 6 hours before serving. Serve with bland crackers.

Yield: 12 servings

Two contributing cooks, Katherine Campbell and Kathy Nolin, separately obtained this recipe from school chums in the early 1980's. They have enjoyed it for two decades.

Sweet and Sour Meatballs

1 pound ground beef	1 (15 ounce) jar Heinz chili sauce
1 egg	
salt and pepper, to taste	1 (8 ounce) jar orange marmalade
1 small-medium onion, chopped fine	
	lemon juice, to taste
1-2 teaspoons parsley flakes	2 tablespoons oil (or less)
½ cup bread crumbs, dry canned	

Make meatballs of about 1½ to 2 inch diameter by mixing first six ingredients together and forming balls by hand. In a crock pot on low, mix together the last three ingredients and allow to simmer. Fry meatballs until browned on all sides and place in sauce in a crock pot and continue to simmer until ready to serve.

Grape or red currant jelly may be used instead of the marmalade. Also, try it with cocktail sausages.

Yield: 6 servings

Deviled Ham Appetizer Quiches

1	package pie crust mix	¼	teaspoon salt
2	eggs, beaten	⅛	teaspoon cayenne
½	cup light cream		pepper
1	(4½ ounce) can deviled	1	tablespoon margarine
	ham	½	cup onion, chopped fine
½	cup Swiss cheese,		
	shredded		

Preheat oven to 450 degrees. Prepare two piecrusts as directed by package (or make own) and roll out to about ¼ inch thick. Using a 3 inch round cookie cutter, cut 32 rounds. Place rounds in bottom of muffin tins. Prick center of each round with a toothpick and bake for 5 minutes at 450 degrees. While these are baking, in a medium bowl, beat the eggs and add to the eggs the cream, ham, cheese, salt, and pepper. Mix well. In a small skillet, melt the margarine and stir in the onions. Add the contents of the bowl to the skillet and combine. Place 1 tablespoon of the completed filling into each pastry and bake at 450 degrees for about 15 minutes.

Yield: 32 mini-quiches

Party Cheese Ball Spread

28	ounces cream cheese, softened	1	tablespoon green bell pepper, chopped fine
2	cups sharp cheddar cheese, shredded	2	teaspoons Worcestershire sauce
1	tablespoon pimiento, chopped	1	teaspoon lemon juice
1	tablespoon onions, chopped fine	1	tablespoon paprika walnuts, finely chopped

Combine softened cream cheese and shredded cheddar cheese, mixing well. Add remaining ingredients except paprika and walnuts. Mix well and chill. Shape into two or more balls and roll balls in paprika and chopped nuts before serving with crackers.

Yield: Two 4 inch balls

Cheeseburger Spice Party Ryes

1	pound ground beef	1	teaspoon garlic, minced
1	pound mild or hot sausage roll	1	teaspoon dried oregano
		1	loaf party rye bread
1	pound processed cheese (such as Velveeta) cut into 1 inch cubes		

Preheat oven to 350 degrees. Sauté ground beef and sausage until brown. Pour off excess grease. Add cheese, garlic and oregano. Heat over low heat until cheese is melted. Cool and spread on individual party rye bread slices. Place slices with spread in a single layer on a baking sheet (may refrigerate covered with kitchen wrap for several hours if needed at this point). Bake at 350 degrees until heated through.

Yield: 30 appetizers

Cheesy Pita Bites

butter	onion, sliced thin
Pita bread or flatbread	Parmesan cheese, grated
canned Italian tomato sauce with basil	

Butter top of Pita or flat bread. Cut into small slices or squares (about 2 x 2 inches). Add sliced onion to top and, with a slotted spoon, place a moderate amount of tomato sauce over the onion. Sprinkle with cheese. Broil or bake in preheated oven at 375 degrees until edges brown.

A fast easy appetizer anytime. You can also just butter the top, slice pita or bread in half, and sprinkle with cheese. Then broil or bake and serve warm or at room temperature in a bread basket for a buffet dinner.

Yield: as much as you care to make

Parmesan-Artichoke Crostini ("Little Toasts")

1   (14 ounce) can
artichoke hearts,
drained and chopped
1   (4½ ounce) can green
chilies, drained and
chopped
2   cloves garlic, minced

1   cup light mayonnaise
1   cup fresh Parmesan
cheese, grated
1   baguette (long, narrow
cylinder of French
bread), sliced into ¼
inch slices and toasted

*am Nance
promises that
this is quick,
easy and
incredibly
delicious.*

Preheat oven to 400 degrees. Stir together all ingredients except the baguette slices. Spread one tablespoon of the mixture on each bread slice. Place on baking sheet and bake at 400 degrees for 3 to 5 minutes or until thoroughly heated.

Yield: 3 dozen

Baked Brie

1   round Brie cheese
1   package of Pillsbury
two pie crust pastries

1   tablespoon orange
marmalade or hot
pepper sweet relish or
lime marmalade
1   egg, beaten

Preheat oven to 375 degrees. Open one pastry and cut a circle in the pastry using the lid of the Brie box. Open other pastry circle. Spread marmalade or relish on one side of the Brie and place it in the center of the uncut, opened larger pastry with the marmalade or relish covered side down. Place smaller cut circle of pastry on top of Brie and fold bottom pastry up and over it, cutting off excess folds of pastry. Turn this pastry covered Brie over and place it on a nonstick baking sheet. Cut out pastry "leaves" from leftover pastry to decorate top of pastry Brie and glaze top with the beaten egg. Bake at 375 degrees for 15 to 20 minutes until pastry is golden. Serve on a plate with crackers (Carr's water biscuits are best).

Yield: 12 to 15 servings

Pimiento Cheese Spread

2 (7 ounce) cans pimiento	1 pound sharp cheddar cheese, grated
1 pound Swiss cheese, grated	1 quart mayonnaise
	1½ tablespoons onion juice

With steel blade in food processor, chop pimiento well. Place chopped pimiento in a bowl and add the cheeses. Combine by hand. Add mayonnaise and onion juice. Mix by hand. Let stand in refrigerator about 48 hours before using.

Yield: 2½ pounds

Because of hand mixing this dish is squishy and fun to make. Vera Evans acquired the original recipe from Mollie Fearing who always made this to serve opening nights at the Lost Colony.

Hearts of Palm Spread

1 (14 ounce) can hearts of palm, drained and chopped	¾ cup mayonnaise
	½ cup Parmesan cheese, fresh grated
1 cup (about 4 ounces) mozzarella cheese, shredded	¼ cup sour cream
	2 tablespoons green onions, minced

Preheat oven to 350 degrees. Combine all ingredients. Spoon into a lightly greased 9 inch quiche dish and bake at 350 degrees for 20 minutes. Serve with crackers.

Yield: 3 cups

3 cups Vidalia onions, finely chopped	
2 cups Swiss cheese, finely chopped	Preheat oven to 350 degrees. Mix all ingredients and spread into a shallow baking or quiche dish. Bake at 350
1 cup mayonnaise	

degrees for 35 minutes and serve with Triscuit crackers.

Yield: 5 cups

This recipe is a favorite of the owners of The Summer Place Bed and Breakfast; Jean and Don Huston.

Spicy Mustard Dip

¼ cup dry mustard
2 tablespoons white vinegar
4 tablespoons water
¼ cup sugar

1 egg yolk, beaten
1 (8 ounce) package cream cheese, room temperature

Combine mustard, vinegar and water in a saucepan. Add sugar and beaten egg yolk. Stir and cook over medium heat until thickened. Let cool. Whip cream cheese into mustard sauce until smooth. Pour into a serving bowl and serve with pretzels.

May use low-fat cream cheese. Also try this with bagel chips.

Yield: 1¼ cups

Some commonly found family names persisting from the 1700's to today on the Outer Banks: Ballance, Baum, Beasley, Bragg, Burrus, Daniels, Etheridge, Gaskins, Gray, Jennette, Meekins, Midgett, Perry, Pugh, Scarborough, Tillett, Tolson, Twiford, Wade, Wallace, Whedbee, and Williams.

Various Sources.

Pris' Hot Vidalia Dip

Tish Leonard loves this dip with Triscuit crackers.

1 cup Vidalia onions, chopped
1 cup mozzarella cheese, shredded

¾ cup real mayonnaise
½ cup Parmesan cheese, grated
¼ cup real sour cream

Preheat oven to 350 degrees. Combine all ingredients. Spoon into a lightly greased 9 inch quiche dish and bake at 350 degrees for about 20 minutes.

Can use any mild type onions, but Vidalia works best as does real mayo and sour cream.

Yield: 3½ cups

Tex-Mex Layered Avocado Spread

2-3 mashed avocados,
　　peeled and pitted
1　lime, juice of
3-4 green onions including
　　green part, chopped
1　cup sour cream
1　cup mild taco sauce
　　(such as El Paso)

½　pound (or up to
　　¾ pound) Monterey
　　Jack cheese, grated
black or green olives,
　　optional garnish
tortilla chips

Layer evenly, in order, all ingredients in a 9 inch glass pie pan. Ensure the avocado paste is spread evenly over bottom of pan, then squeeze lime juice over this and tilt so juice spreads and runs over the avocados. Be sure all layers come all the way to the pan's edges. Cover with plastic wrap and refrigerate. Serve with tortilla chips.

Can be made up early on the night to be served.

Yield: 10 to 12 servings

Microwave "Trash"

½　cup canola oil
1　teaspoon garlic powder,
　　heaping
¼　teaspoon (or less)
　　cayenne pepper
1　teaspoon
　　Worcestershire sauce
2　cups pretzel sticks

2　cups Wheat Chex cereal
2　cups original Frito's or
　　"Bugles"
2　cups Cheeze Its or
　　cheese tid-bit crackers
2½ cups peanuts
2　tablespoons dry
　　Parmesan cheese,
　　grated

Mix first four ingredients in a bowl. Put remaining ingredients, except for Parmesan cheese, in a 3 quart microwave safe dish. Stir bowl mixture and pour slowly over dry mixture, stirring as you pour. Sprinkle with Parmesan cheese and stir again. Microwave on high for 6 to 8 minutes, stirring every 2 minutes. Cool and store in an airtight container.

Yield: about 10 cups

Granddaughter Chelsea's Yogurt Dip for Fruit

This recipe is one submitted by Louise Fields for her young granddaughter, Chelsea Heslin, age six.

1 cup thawed Cool Whip Lite

1 (8 ounce) container strawberry low-fat yogurt

½ cup chopped strawberries, sweetened to taste

Mix all ingredients well and chill. Serve as a dip with fresh fruits.

Yield: about 2½ cups

Mama's Potato Soup for Crock Pots

A McDermott favorite, sufficient for a family of four with enough left to send a large bowl to friends.

6 potatoes, peeled and cut into bite-size pieces

2 leeks, sliced into ¼ inch pieces

2 onions, chopped

1 carrot, peeled and sliced

1 stalk celery, sliced

4 bouillon cubes, vegetable or beef

1 tablespoon parsley flakes

5 cups water

1 tablespoon salt
   pepper, to taste

⅓ cup butter

1 (12 ounce) can evaporated milk

chives, chopped to garnish, optional

Put all ingredients except evaporated milk and chives into a 5 quart crock pot. Cover and cook on low for 10 to 12 hours, or on high for 4 to 5 hours. Stir in evaporated milk the last hour. If desired, mash potatoes up before serving and sprinkle each serving with chopped chives for garnish.

For a family dinner, serve soup with cheddar cheese toast and a tossed salad.

Yield: 10 to 12 servings

Cream of Potato-Leek Soup

4	leeks	2	cups milk
¼	cup butter	2	cups half-and-half
1	large onion, cut in half then sliced		fresh chives, garnish optional and to taste
5	cups chicken broth (homemade, please)		cracked black pepper, garnish optional and to taste
2	teaspoons salt		
3	pounds potatoes, peeled and sliced thin (recommend red bliss potatoes)		

Come, Lord Jesus, be our guest, and may our meal by you be blest.

Martin Luther, 1483-1546.

Remove and discard green tops of leeks. Cut white portion of leeks into thin slices. Melt butter in a Dutch oven over medium-high heat. Add leeks and onion and sauté until tender, about 5 minutes. Stir in broth, salt and potatoes. Cover and reduce heat to simmer. Simmer 35 to 40 minutes. Cool slightly. In a food processor, process or blend in small batches until smooth. Return this mixture to the Dutch oven. Stir in milk and half-and-half. Cook over medium heat, stirring often, until thoroughly heated. Do not boil. Garnish, if desired.

Freezes well before adding the milks.

Yield: 5 quarts

Fresh Tomato Broth

2	cups beef broth	¼	cup dry white vermouth
2	large ripe tomatoes, skins on	4	parsley sprigs, no stems
		1	whole lemon rind, grated

Share with God's people who are in need. Practice hospitality.

Romans 12:13.

Bring broth to a boil in a saucepan. Reduce heat and simmer for 5 minutes. Slice tomatoes into pan. Add vermouth, parsley and lemon rind. Cook on low for six minutes. Purée in a blender and serve hot.

Chill the purée soup and serve cold, adding a shot of vodka.

Yield: 2 servings

Warming Squash Soup

2 large butternut squash	2 large Granny Smith apples, peeled, cored and chopped
6 tablespoons (¾ stick) butter	salt and fresh ground pepper, to taste
2 yellow onions, chopped	
8 fresh sage leaves, shredded	fresh grated nutmeg, optional to taste
6 cups low-sodium chicken broth	sour cream "dollop" garnish, optional

Preheat oven to 400 degrees. Prick each squash with the tip of a knife, place squash on baking sheets and roast until a knife penetrates the squash with ease, about 1 hour. Let squash cool and then cut squash lengthwise, scoop out seeds and fibers to discard. Reserve the pulp by scooping it out in chunks and placing pulp in a bowl. In a saucepan over medium heat, melt butter, add onions and half the sage. Cook stirring occasionally until onions are tender, about 8 to 10 minutes. Add broth and squash pulp. Increase heat to high and bring to a boil. Reduce heat to low and simmer. Stir every 3 to 4 minutes. Using a hand blender purée soup directly in the pan, adding chopped apples also to be puréed. If using an electric blender or food processor, add apples to soup, blend to a purée and return soup to pan. Reheat gently over medium-low heat. Soup should be a creamy bisque-like consistency. Season with salt, pepper and nutmeg, if desired, to taste. Ladle into warmed soup bowls and garnish with a dollop of sour cream and the rest of the sage leaves, if desired.

This soup has unlimited variations depending on the cook's taste and sense of adventure. Try adding or changing spices. Curry spices go with it quite well. Cream, plain water or orange juice can be substituted for the broth or try equal parts water and coconut milk.

Yield: 6 servings

White Bean and Beer Soup

¾ cup onion, chopped	1 teaspoon salt
¼ cup carrots, finely chopped	¼ teaspoon black pepper, freshly ground
3 tablespoons olive oil	1 teaspoon Worcestershire sauce
28 ounces navy beans, canned	1 cup water
½ cup tomatoes, chopped	½ cup beer

Sauté onions and carrots in the oil for five minutes in a large deep skillet. Add beans, tomatoes, seasonings and water. Simmer for 20 minutes. Place one cup of soup in blender and purée. Place purée back into rest of soup and add the beer. Stir and serve. Give remaining beer to the cook.

Yield: 3 servings

Father high in heaven, all by you are fed; Hear your children thank you for our daily bread. You send sun and showers, birds sing overhead, While the corn is growing for our daily bread.

Unknown.

Creamy Peanut Soup

3 cups chicken broth	peanuts, chopped, optional garnish
1 cup peanut butter, smooth style	sour cream, optional garnish
1 teaspoon seasoned salt	paprika, optional garnish
1⅓ cups cream, or 1 (13 ounce) can evaporated milk	

Over high heat, bring broth to a boil. Lower heat and add peanut butter. Blend until smooth. Add salt. Keeping heat low, stir in cream or milk. Heat but do not boil. Top with chopped peanuts or a dollop of sour cream or sprinkle with paprika.

For a thicker soup, 2 tablespoons flour may be slowly added to the broth as it initially heats. Some of our cooks brown 2 ribs of chopped celery and 1 small chopped onion in butter and also add that to the initial broth and strain it before adding the peanut butter.

Yield: 4 to 6 servings

Bermuda-Style Crock Pot Fish Chowder

𝐵ruce Nolin says "This is the only way I can get my wife to eat fish chowder because all the other recipes are 'too fishy' for her. It also freezes well."

6	fish heads, or 4 fish fillets	2	tablespoons salt
3	large onions, chopped	1	teaspoon thyme
8	stalks celery, chopped	3	bay leaves
1	clove garlic, chopped	1	teaspoon whole peppercorns
2	tablespoons butter	1	teaspoon ground cloves
2	pounds potatoes, cubed	2	teaspoons parsley
5-6	carrots, sliced	2	tablespoons Worcestershire sauce
28	ounces canned tomatoes, undrained	½	teaspoon curry powder
12	ounces beef consommé		black rum or sherry, optional to taste
1	cup ketchup		Gravy Master, optional to taste and color
1	lemon, juice of		

In a crock pot, or kettle, simmer fish or fish heads with water until meat leaves bones. Remove bones. Reserve fish meat. Sauté onions, celery and garlic until soft. In a clean crock pot or kettle, place cooked fish, sautéed vegetables and all other ingredients and cook on low or simmer for a minimum of six to a maximum of ten hours, stirring occasionally. Add optional ingredients to taste and color broth as desired.

Yield: about 16 servings

Anna's Fish Soup

3	fish fillets, deboned (grouper, sheepshead or puppy drum) water, lightly salted	1	small onion, diced
		1	cup water, no salt
		2	medium potatoes, peeled and diced
3	carrots, grated	1	cup milk
3	stalks celery, diced	2	teaspoons butter

Simmer fish in lightly salted water to cover until done. Remove fish from water and strain stock. Add carrots, celery and onion and 1 cup water to strained stock and bring to a boil. Crumble fish meat into small pieces and add to stock, reducing heat to medium and stirring often. Make sure liquid covers the ingredients, adding water as needed. Over medium heat, bring to boiling and then simmer 5 minutes. Add potatoes and simmer until potatoes are done, about 20 minutes. Remove from heat and let cool 30 minutes. Add milk and butter. Reheat slowly for approximately 10 minutes until warmed.

Yield: 8 servings

While fishing in Florida, Anna Sadler and her "snowbird" friends competed to invent new ways to cook tasty fish. This recipe made it to the number one place. Easy to prepare, no strange ingredients, nutritious, done in less than an hour and freezes well.

Hobo Stew or "Slumgullion"

4 slices bacon, diced
1 medium onion
1 (16 ounce) can tomatoes
2 (16 ounce) cans red
kidney beans, drained
1 (15 ounce) can corn
1 (4 ounce) can
mushroom pieces

1 (12 ounce) can
mushroom gravy
2 tablespoons chili
powder
½ pound cheddar cheese,
grated
1 pound franks, each
frank cut into 6 pieces

This is a tradition at Betsy Steketee's house every April 15 after the tax returns are in the mail.

Fry bacon until crisp and drain on paper towels, reserving 1 tablespoon of grease. Set bacon aside and cook onion in bacon fat until golden brown. Transfer to large kettle and add tomatoes, beans, corn, mushrooms, gravy and chili powder. Mix well and bring to a boil. Reduce heat and add cheese. Stir until cheese melts. Add franks and reserved bacon (may thin with water or more tomato juice if soup looks too thick). Heat through and ladle into serving bowls, dividing franks evenly.

Yield: 6 to 8 servings

Kielbasa Soup

8	ounces (about ½ a ring) Kielbasa, cut into bite-size chunks	8-10	ounces frozen mixed vegetables, peas or green beans
2	tablespoons light olive oil	1	(12 ounce) can evaporated milk, regular or skim
1	stalk celery, coarsely sliced	1	tablespoon Worcestershire sauce
1-5	garlic cloves, to taste		
1	small to medium onion, in chunks	1	(11 ounce) can corn, vacuum packed (no water or juice)
½	cup water		
4	medium potatoes, peeled and in chunks		Tabasco sauce, to taste

𝒲hat God gives, and what he takes, is a gift for Jesus' sake; be the meal of beans or peas, we thank God for those and these.

Robert Herrick, 1591-1674.

Sauté Kielbasa (recommend Hillshire Farms Lite Kielbasa turkey, beef or pork) in olive oil with celery, garlic and onion in a kettle. Add ½ cup water and potatoes. Cook on medium 10 minutes. Add frozen vegetables and cook another 10 minutes on medium. Add milk, Worcestershire sauce, corn and a few drops of Tabasco sauce. Heat through (do not boil). If not enough broth add another ½ cup water. When potatoes are done, serve.

A very hearty soup, best served on a very cold day.

Yield: 6 to 8 servings

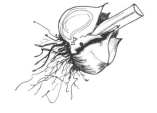

Italian Soup

1 pound lean ground beef or beef tips	1 tablespoon chili powder, optional
1 medium onion, chopped	1 (16 ounce) can kidney beans, drained
2 (14½ ounce) cans Italian tomatoes	1 (16 ounce) can Italian green beans, drained
1 (10¾ ounce) can tomato soup with basil	1 carrot, chopped
4 cups water	1 zucchini, chopped
2 cloves garlic, minced	8 ounces rotini noodles, cooked per package directions
2 teaspoons dried basil	
2 teaspoons dried oregano	grated Parmesan cheese, to garnish
1 teaspoon salt	
½ teaspoon pepper	

Cook beef and onion in a Dutch oven on medium heat, stirring until beef crumbles and/or is no longer pink. Drain off juices. Stir in tomatoes, soup, water and seasonings including chili powder if desired. Bring to a boil. Reduce heat and simmer, stirring occasionally, for 30 minutes. Stir in both types of beans, carrots and zucchini. Simmer another 15 minutes, stirring occasionally. Stir in cooked pasta. Serve with cheese for garnish.

Yield: 10 to 12 servings

Van's Tex-Mex Stew

1½ pound lean pork, cubed	2 carrots, thinly sliced into 1 inch strips
2 tablespoons olive oil	2 small cans (4.5 ounces each) green chilies or to taste
1 large onion, chopped	
4 cloves garlic, minced	
2 (15 ounce) cans chicken broth	coarse ground black pepper
2 (15 ounce) cans hominy, white or yellow	juice of 1 lime
1 green or red bell pepper, chopped	

Brown pork in olive oil with onion and garlic. Place in 4 quart pot with chicken broth and simmer for 1 hour. Add hominy along with its liquid, bell pepper, carrots and green chilies with juice. Add black pepper to taste and simmer for another hour. Just before serving add the lime juice.

Yield: 4 to 6 servings

This recipe is shared by an old friend of Frank and Nancy Maturo, Van Greene, a native Texan who enjoys cooking and entertaining " Texas-style" with his wife, Vonda.

Virginia's Summer Tea-Light

water	1 (12 ounce) frozen lemonade concentrate
4 family size tea bags	
¾ cup granulated sugar (more may be added to taste)	

In a quart of water, brew a pot of strong tea using the 4 tea bags. Remove the tea bags and dissolve the sugar in the tea. In a gallon-sized container, mix the sweetened tea, lemonade concentrate, and enough water to fill the container.

Yield: 1 gallon

Frank and Nancy Maturo say "Our drink of choice in the summer. This is from an old family recipe of a dear friend, Virginia Watson."

Ice Tea "Syrup"

5 cups boiling water	2 cups granulated sugar
5 tablespoons loose tea leaves	

Betsy Steketee says this syrup keeps well even when refrigerated for several weeks and is very convenient in hot weather.

Pour boiling water over tea leaves and allow to stand 7 to 10 minutes. Strain out leaves and pour hot tea over sugar. Stir until all sugar is dissolved. Cool and store in refrigerator. To serve, pour about one inch of syrup into a tall glass, add ice and water. Stir.

Yield: 20 tall glasses

Spring Party Punch

3 cups water	1 (6 ounce) can frozen lemonade concentrate, thawed
1 cup granulated sugar	
2 ripe bananas cut in half	2 tablespoons fresh lemon juice
3 cups unsweetened pineapple juice	
1 (16 ounce) can frozen orange juice concentrate, thawed	52 ounces club soda or lemon-lime soda
	orange slices, lemon slices, maraschino cherries for garnish

"A few families salted mullet or dried the brittle stems and waxy leaves of the yaupon bushes to make tea. They traded the mullet and tea on the mainland for corn to be ground in one of seven windmills on the cape. But as late as the Civil War a visitor to Hatteras Island would write that the residents 'seldom see money, indeed they have no use for it.'"

From Hatteras Journal *by Jan DeBlieu, 1987.*

Several days before serving, combine water and sugar in saucepan. Bring to boil and stir until sugar is dissolved. Remove from stove and cool. In a blender or processor combine the bananas and half the pineapple juice. Blend until smooth. Stir in the sugar water and rest of the juices. If used, add rum and blend well. Freeze in zip-lock plastic storage bags (keeps well for several months). Just before the party, place frozen mixture in punch bowl adding the soda. Stir gently to combine. Add garnish.

May replace the 52 ounces of soda with 1½ cups rum and 32 ounces of soda.

Yield: 25 (4 ounce) servings, non alcohol, or 21 (4 ounce) rum version

Spicy Fruit Punch

2 cups orange juice	½ teaspoon mixed spice or ground allspice
2 cups pineapple juice	
juice and rind of one lemon	6 cloves
1 cup water	2 cups chilled Lipton Soothing Moments Orange and Spice Tea (made with two tea bags)
¾ cup granulated sugar	
½ teaspoon nutmeg	
	4 cups ginger ale

Mix the orange, pineapple and lemon juice in a pitcher or jug and set aside. In a saucepan, mix water, sugar, lemon rind, and spices. Heat to a simmer for 10 minutes. Cool. Add to cold tea and ginger ale. Blend into the pitcher or jug of fruit juices. Add crushed ice before serving.

Yield: 11 (8 ounce glass) or 22 (4 ounce punch cup) servings

Come, all you who are thirsty, come to the waters; and you who have no money, come, buy and eat! Come, buy wine and milk without money and without cost.

Isaiah 55:1.

Lemony Light Cooler

3 cups white grape juice or one 750 ml bottle dry white wine, chilled	½ cup lemon juice
	1 (32 ounce) bottle club soda, chilled
½ cup granulated sugar (more may be added to taste)	lemon, lime, orange, strawberry slices or other fresh fruit
	ice

In pitcher, combine grape juice or wine, sugar and lemon juice. Stir until sugar dissolves.

Cover and chill. Just before serving, add club soda and fruit. Serve over ice.

Recipe can be doubled as needed.

Yield: 7 cups

Sangría Slush

1 (20 ounce) can pineapple chunks in juice, drained	¼ cup plus 2 tablespoons frozen lemonade concentrate, thawed
2 (11 ounce) cans mandarin oranges in light syrup, drained	1 cup club soda, chilled orange rind curls to garnish
2 cups burgundy or other dry red wine, chilled	

This recipe is from a dear friend of the Maturos's, Lindsey Ein of Lexington, KY, who often visits them on the Outer Banks. When they visit her, she is a delightful hostess and gourmet cook, willing to share her secrets.

Set aside 8 pineapple chunks. Place remaining pineapple and mandarin oranges on a baking sheet. Freeze 2 hours or until firm. Place knife blade in food processor bowl, add frozen fruit and process for 30 seconds. Add half (one cup) wine and lemonade concentrate. Process until smooth. Pour into large pitcher. Add remaining wine and club soda. Stir well. Pour into individual glasses garnishing each with reserved pineapple chunk and orange rind curl. Serve immediately.

Yield: 8 (6 ounce glass) servings or 12 (four ounce punch cup) servings

Whiskey Sour Punch

cherries, lemon slices, lime slices frozen in water in a Bundt pan to make an ice ring	6 ounces frozen orange juice concentrate, thawed and undiluted
12 ounces frozen lemonade concentrate, thawed and undiluted	67 ounces ginger ale (or 7-Up or lemon-lime soda)
	2 cups bourbon (or more, to taste)

Place fruited ice ring into a punch bowl. Pour thawed concentrates into punch bowl and dilute with ginger ale or soda. Add bourbon.

Ice ring thaws slower than ice cubes and adds flavor of the fruit as it thaws.

Yield: 24 (4 ounce punch cup) servings

Cranberry Punch

5	quarts cranberry juice	2	(32 ounce) cans Dole
1	(16 ounce) orange juice frozen concentrate		pineapple juice
		4	(2 liter) bottles ginger
2	(16 ounce) lemonade frozen concentrate		ale

Chill all liquids before mixing in large bowl. Serve over ice or float an ice ring with cherries frozen into it.

Yield: 80 (4 ounce) servings

"I made this adjusted to the number of guests many times most recently to celebrate my cousin's one hundredth birthday. It was so popular it ran out long before the food did, with many compliments received!" states Vera Evans.

Boy Scout Cocoa

1	large (30 ounce) Nestle or Hershey Quick Cocoa powder mix	1	pound 10X or granulated sugar
1	(14 ounce) dried milk mix	1	(10 or 12 ounce) jar of non-dairy creamer (such as Cremora)
4	ounces cocoa powder		

Mix all ingredients in large container with tight seal. To serve, place 2 tablespoons of the mixture in an 8 ounce cup. Add only enough water to moisten. Then add hot water. Stir.

Milk may be used instead of water and the milk plus mixture slowly warmed.

Yield: a gallon

Lou Overman says that this is an economical and easy to "pack" mix for camping trips and large gatherings on cool nights.

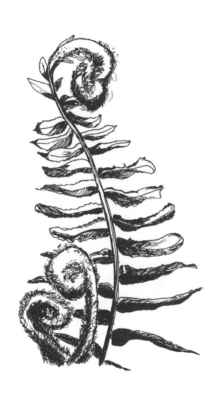

Breads and Spreads

Breads, Rolls, Muffins,
Biscuits, Jams and Jellies

Kerry Oaksmith-Sanders

Loaves and Fishes

"We have here but five loaves, and two fishes"
—Matthew 14:17

At the end of the long day, when the disciples wanted to send everybody home, Jesus told them not to be ridiculous, that the people were tired and hungry. "But we only have five loaves of bread and two fishes, barely enough for ourselves," the disciples argued. "How can we feed that many?" "Give me what you have," Jesus told them. Then Jesus looked up to Heaven, offered thanks, blessed the food, and gave it back to the disciples to distribute. Miraculously, after everyone had finished eating as much as they wanted, twelve baskets of leftovers remained.

As long as you have a few loaves and fishes, and know what to do with them, all you have is all you need.

Irish Soda Bread

4	cups flour	6	tablespoons unsalted butter
3	tablespoons sugar		
1	tablespoon baking powder	2	tablespoons caraway seeds
1	teaspoon salt	1½	cups raisins
1	teaspoon baking soda	2	eggs
		1½	cups buttermilk

Preheat oven to 350 degrees. Mix flour and next four ingredients. With a pastry blender or butter knife, cut in butter until mixture resembles coarse crumbs. Add caraway seeds and raisins. In a separate bowl, beat eggs. Reserve 2 tablespoons of the beaten eggs. Stir buttermilk in remaining eggs and then into flour mixture until dough is moistened. Dough will be sticky. Turn dough onto a floured surface and with floured hands, knead for about 10 strokes to mix thoroughly. Shape into two equal balls and place on a greased cookie sheet. Cut about a ¾ inch deep cross into the top of each ball and brush with the reserved beaten egg. Bake at 350 degrees for about 40 minutes, until inserted knife in center comes out clean. Cool on a wire rack.

Yield: 2 round loaves

Don't you know that a little yeast works through the whole batch of dough? Get rid of the old yeast that you may be a new batch without yeast — as you already are. For Christ, our Passover lamb, has been sacrificed. Therefore let us keep the Festival, not with the old yeast, the yeast of malice and wickedness, but with bread without yeast, the bread of sincerity and truth.

1 Corinthians 5: 6-8.

Mom's Cracked Wheat Bread

2 cups boiling water	1 tablespoon salt
2 cups cracked wheat	2 packages active dry
½ cup honey or brown	yeast (softened in
sugar	½ cup warm water)
2 tablespoons butter	5 cups (or 5½ cups if
	desired) flour

Combine boiling water and cracked wheat, honey (or brown sugar), butter and salt in a large bowl. Cool to warm. Prepare the yeast in the warm water and combine with large bowl ingredients. Beat in 4 cups of flour, then knead in remaining flour (1 to 1½ cups). Cover top of bowl with damp towel and allow dough to rise to double the original amount. When risen, punch down and then shape into loaves in greased pans. Preheat oven to 400 degrees. Allow to rise again. Bake at 400 degrees for about 40 minutes.

May substitute the 2 cups cracked wheat with 1¾ cups cracked wheat and ¼ cup Bulghur wheat, or you may use wheat germ in place of the Bulghur wheat.

Yield: 4 loaves

Pauline's Corn-Style Bread

1 stick (½ cup) margarine	1 (12 ounce) package
1 (8 ounce) package	muffin mix (such as
cream cheese	Flako)
3 eggs	1 (16 ounce) can cream
2 tablespoons sugar	style corn

Preheat oven to 400 degrees. Beat margarine, cream cheese eggs and sugar together. Add muffin mix and corn. Mix well. Bake in lightly greased 9 x 13 inch baking dish at 400 degrees for 25 minutes.

Yield: 12 servings

My Sister's 1950's North Carolina Bishop's Bread

3	eggs, well beaten	1	(10 ounce) jar maraschino cherries, drained and chopped
3	tablespoons butter		
1	cup sugar		
1½	cup flour	1	(6 ounce) package semi-sweet chocolate pieces
1½	teaspoons baking powder		
½	teaspoon salt	1	cup pecans, chopped coarsely
1	cup dates, chopped		

Cream eggs and butter together and then add the sugar, mixing well. In a separate bowl, sift together the flour, baking powder and salt. Add to this the creamed egg mixture and stir in dates, cherries, chocolate pieces and nuts. Pour batter into a well greased 9 x 5 x 3 inch loaf pan and bake in a slow oven, 325 degrees, for 1½ hours or until cake tester comes out clean from center. Allow to cool in pan for 10 minutes. Turn out on wire rack to finish cooling, then wrap in foil to let it "rest" overnight before serving.

Yield: 1 loaf

Lou Overman makes this sometimes as a great Christmas gift. It is especially good served thinly sliced with thin slices of a sharp cheese.

Walnut Bread

5½ cups flour (to be used in 1 cup, ½ cup and 4 cup portions)

1½ teaspoons salt

1 package dry active yeast

1⅓ cup water

¼ cup milk

¼ cup molasses

¼ cup (4 tablespoons) butter or margarine

1 egg

1 cup old-fashioned rolled oats

⅔ cup walnuts, chopped

Original recipe by Lydia Malco and submitted by Patty Johnson

In a large bowl, combine 1 cup flour with the salt and yeast. In a saucepan, combine the water, milk, molasses and margarine and heat on low until warm. Add this to the flour, salt, yeast bowl and beat with an electric mixer on medium speed for 2 minutes. Add the egg, oats and ½ cup flour and beat an additional 2 minutes on high speed. Add the remaining 4 cups of flour and nuts and stir by hand until stiff and well combined. Knead for 8 to 10 minutes and then let rise in a lightly greased bowl covered by a damp towel for 1 hour. Punch down and divide equally between two loaf pans. Cover again and let rise a second time for 75 minutes. Bake in a preheated 400 degree oven for 30 minutes. Remove from oven and let cool 3 to 5 minutes, then remove from pans and continue to cool on wire rack.

Yield: 2 loaves

Outer Banks Hush Puppies

2	cups cornmeal	1	tablespoon baking powder
1	cup regular flour		minced onion, to taste (optional)
2	cups water		oil rated for high temperature cooking (such as peanut or safflower oil)
1	cup canned evaporated milk		
2	eggs, beaten smooth		
2	tablespoons sugar		
1	teaspoon salt		

Mix all ingredients. Heat sufficient oil in a deep pot such that dropped spoonfuls of batter will sink into the hot oil. When oil is hot enough to deep fry, drop in spoonfuls of batter. After 2 to 3 minutes they will rise to the top and are done. Remove with a slotted spoon and drain on paper towels.

Test the oil temperature with one spoonful of batter. If it rises in 2 to 3 minutes, the oil is hot enough.

Yield: 4 to 6 servings

Without these, no fried seafood or fish dinner is complete on the Outer Banks.

Broccoli Cornbread

¼	pound (1 stick) margarine, melted	1	(8 ounce) box cornbread mix (such as Jiffy)
1	(12 ounce) carton cottage cheese	1	(10 ounce) package frozen chopped broccoli, thawed and drained
4	eggs		
1	medium onion, chopped		

Preheat oven to 400 degrees. In a 2 quart (8 x 12 inch) oven safe baking dish, place the melted butter, and then mix in, one at a time, in order as listed, the remaining ingredients. Bake at 400 degrees for 25 to 30 minutes or until top is golden brown.

Yield: 8 servings

Scones

1⅓	cups shortening	¼	teaspoon salt
1½	cups powdered sugar	4	teaspoons baking soda
4	eggs	3½	cups cold milk
10	cups flour	1	cup currants or dried
3	tablespoons cream of		cranberries
	tartar		

Preheat oven to 400 degrees. Cream together the shortening and powdered sugar until light. Stir in eggs until thoroughly blended. In a separate bowl, sift together the flour, cream of tartar and salt. In a third bowl mix the baking soda with the cold milk. Combine creamed mixture with the flour mixture. Add the milk mixture and mix thoroughly. Fold in the currants or cranberries. Roll out dough on a floured surface to about 1½ inch thickness. Cut scones with a biscuit cutter dipped in flour. Place on greased baking sheets placing the scones about 2 inches apart. You may want to take an additional egg, beat it lightly and brush the top of the scones with it, but this is optional. Bake the scones at 400 degrees for 15 to 25 minutes.

Yield: 4 dozen

Aunt Myrt's Heavenly Biscuits

This recipe was rediscovered by Lou Overman in a Bible of a deceased relative, Martha Newsome Lassiter. Easy to make and a family favorite.

1	cup sifted self rising	2	tablespoons mayonnaise
	flour	½	cup sweet (whole) milk

Preheat oven to 400 degrees. Mix ingredients thoroughly. Drop into very lightly greased muffin tins by spoon to make six biscuits. Bake at 400 degrees until light brown.

Yield: 6 biscuits

Win's Potato Rolls

2-3 potatoes (enough to make 1 cup cooked and mashed)

2-3 cups water

1-2 packages active dry yeast (two packages speeds up the rising)

⅔ cup sugar

1 cup butter or margarine, melted

4 eggs, well beaten

2 teaspoons salt

6 cups flour (about enough to make a soft dough)

Peel potatoes and cube them. Boil in water until of mashing consistency. Reserving 1½ cups of the potato water, drain the potatoes. Mash potatoes well in a large bowl. Let the reserved potato water cool to lukewarm, then add it, the yeast and the sugar to the potatoes. Be sure the water is not too hot as it will kill the yeast. Combine thoroughly and let stand in a warm place until spongy, about ½ to 1 hour. When this is ready, combine the next four ingredients in a separate bowl to form a soft dough. Stir this dough into the sponge. Mix thoroughly (an electric mixer with dough hook works well), cover and let stand until it rises to double the original bulk, about 2 to 3 hours. Turn risen dough onto a floured surface and knead lightly. Flatten to about an inch thickness and cut into circles with a 2½ inch cutter or water glass or clean and empty soup can. Place on greased cookie sheet, about two inches apart and let rise again for about ½ hour. Bake in a preheated 425 degree oven for 10 to 15 minutes, until pale golden brown. Serve hot, if possible.

If you refrigerate the risen dough (after the first rising and before turning it out to flatten and cut) for 4 to 6 hours it is easier to work.

Keep rolls in freezer for last minute reheating.

Yield: 4 dozen rolls

Once someone has these rolls they never want another variety. Win Jacques says that strong women have been known to weep for joy when first biting into one of these.

Oatmeal Muffins

1 cup regular rolled oats
1 cup buttermilk
½ cup brown sugar, firmly packed
½ cup vegetable oil

1 egg, beaten
1 cup all-purpose flour
1 teaspoon baking powder
½ teaspoon baking soda
½ teaspoon salt

Combine oats and buttermilk. Let stand 1 hour. Preheat oven to 400 degrees. Add sugar, oil eggs and mix completely. In a separate bowl, combine flour, baking powder, baking soda, and salt. Stir in the first wet mixture slowly, adding the wet mixture only until the final product becomes well moistened and not stiff, but also not watery (a little thicker than cake batter). Fill muffin tins ⅔ full and bake at 400 degrees for 20 to 25 minutes.

Yield: 1 dozen muffins

Giant Puff Pastry

1 (9 to 10 inch diameter) sauté pan or skillet, safe for baking in a very hot oven
3 tablespoons unsalted butter

2 eggs
½ cup flour
½ cup milk
¼ cup Gruyère cheese, grated

Preheat oven to 475 to 500 degrees. Melt butter in pan in oven. Remove melted butter, leaving oven on. While butter is being melted, blend eggs, flour, and milk in a blender. Pour the hot melted butter, immediately upon removal of pan from oven into the blender and blend briefly. Pour blender contents back into the pan, sprinkle with the grated cheese and return pan to oven. Bake at 475 to 500 degrees for 10 to 12 minutes. Puff should be dark brown and crusty outside and soft inside.

Yield: 2 servings

"New Friends and Old Friends"
by J. Parry
Make new friends,
but keep the old;
Those are silver,
these are gold.
New-made
friendships, like
new wine,
Age will mellow
and refine.
Friendships that
have stood
the test —
Time and change
— are surely best;
Brow may wrinkle,
hair grow gray,
Friendship never
knows decay.
For 'mid old
friends, tried
and true,
Once more we
our youth renew.
But old friends,
alas! May die,
New friends must
their place supply.
Cherish friendship
in your breast —
New is good,
but old is best;
Make new friends,
but keep the old;
Those are silver,
these are gold.

Leslie's Gram Mac's Muffins

¼ cup butter
¼ cup sugar
2 cups flour
2 teaspoons baking powder
1 egg
¾ cup milk

1 cup chopped dates (optional)
1 cup (or 1½ cups) canned blueberries in juice, drained (optional)
¾ cup miniature chocolate chips (optional)

Preheat oven to 375 degrees. Mix butter, sugar, flour and baking powder with an electric mixer on high speed. When fluffy, add the egg and milk. Beat until smooth. Do not over beat. Stir in your choice of either dates or blueberries or chocolate chips. Pour into greased muffin tins, about ⅔ full, and bake at 375 degrees for 15 to 20 minutes.

Yield: 1 dozen muffins

"As surely as the Lord your God lives," she replied [to Elijah], *"I don't have any bread - only a handful of flour in a jar and a little oil in a jug. I am gathering a few sticks to take home and make a meal for myself and my son, that we may eat it - and die."*

Elijah said to her, "Don't be afraid. Go home and do as you have said. But first make a small cake of bread for me from what you have and bring it to me, and then make something for yourself and your son. For this is what the Lord, the God of Israel, says: 'The jar of flour will not be used up and the jug of oil will not run dry until the day the Lord gives rain on the land.'"

She went away and did as Elijah had told her. So there was food every day for Elijah and for the woman and her family. For the jar of flour was not used up and the jug of oil did not run dry, in keeping with the word of the Lord spoken by Elijah.

1 Kings 17:12-16.

Aunt Cora's Delicious Rhubarb Jam

3   cups chopped
   rhubarb
3   cups sugar

1   (4 ounce) package
   strawberry flavored
   gelatin

Combine rhubarb and sugar in heavy saucepan, and over medium heat, bring to a boil. Boil for 10 minutes exactly and no more, stirring occasionally. Remove from heat and add gelatin. Mix thoroughly and divide into sterilized storage jars with tight covers. Re-tighten when thoroughly cooled.

Yield: 6 pints

"Aunt Cora was an unmarried lady who lived to be 97 years old. Every summer, she made this jam," says Betsy Steketee.

Grape Hull Preserves

scuppernong (or other)
   grapes
granulated white sugar

jelly jars and lids,
   sterilized

Separate hulls from pulp by popping the grapes individually with your finger and popping the pulp into one pan and the hulls in a second pan. Heat, bringing to a simmer slowly, the pulp in a sauce pan, then strain through a colander to remove the seeds. Take the saucepan with the hulls in it and pour the resulting macerated pulp and juices over the hulls. Cover and heat to a simmer. Simmer until hulls are tender when tested with a fork. Add, for each resulting cup of cooked hulls and juice, ¾ cup sugar. Bring the hulls, juice and sugar slowly to a boil, uncovered, and stir occasionally until the hulls are clear or translucent. Pour into sterilized jelly jars and seal tightly. When thoroughly cool, tighten lid or rim.

Yield: as much as you care to make

Lou Overman's mother was a native of Southern Virginia and was raised by her grandmother who handed down this recipe. It was a Christmas tradition of Lou's childhood. These preserves are used to make another recipe in this book, Grape Hull Pie.

Jim Iacone's Peach Marmalade

6	ounces frozen orange juice concentrate, undiluted	1	naval orange rind, slivered
½	cup lemon juice	6	cups granulated sugar
4-5	pounds fresh peaches	1	teaspoon salt

Combine orange juice concentrate and lemon juice in a large mixing bowl. Peel peaches and dice them into this mixture as they are cut to prevent browning of peaches. Measure to ensure there are 8 cups of diced peaches and set peaches in juice mixture aside. Sliver orange rind by cutting thin slices of rind from top to bottom of orange. Place 4 to 5 slices on top each other and cut across to make ⅛ inch slivers. Repeat with remaining rind. Mix peaches and citrus juices with slivered rind, sugar and salt in a 5 to 6 quart pan. Stirring continuously, heat to boiling while spooning off foam as it forms. When foam formation subsides, set burner control so jam cooks at a constant, gentle boil. Stirring occasionally, continue boiling uncovered for 20 to 25 minutes and remove any additional foam. Place a clean, small plate or saucer in the freezer to use to test jam. Jam is finished when about half a teaspoon, chilled on the cold plate, forms a soft gel. Ladle finished, hot jam into sterilized jars, filling to the brim. Clean any sticky; residue away from threaded tops of jars to allow a good seal. Cap immediately and screw lids on tight. Wipe jars clean and invert on a rack to cool.

Yield: 7 half-pint jars of marmalade

Jim Iacone

Yet he gave a command to the skies above and opened the doors of the heavens; he rained down manna for the people to eat, he gave them the grain of heaven. Men ate the bread of angels; he sent them all the food they could eat.

Psalm 78: 23-25.

Jim Iacone's Apple Butter

8	cups apple cider	½	teaspoon ground
1	teaspoon salt		cardamom, optional
2½	teaspoons ground	2	lemons, juice of
	cinnamon	½	cup frozen orange juice
½	teaspoon ground cloves		concentrate,
½	teaspoon ground		undiluted
	allspice	1-2	cups water
½	teaspoon grated	6	pounds Granny Smith
	nutmeg		apples
		3-4	cups granulated sugar

Put cider into a 5 to 6 quart pan and bring to a boil. Continue boiling, stirring occasionally and then more frequently as volume decreases, until cider is reduced to approximately ⅓ its original volume. In a separate small bowl, combine salt, cinnamon, cloves, allspice, nutmeg, and cardamom (if used) and set aside. In another large bowl, combine lemon juice, orange juice, and about 1 cup of water. Peel and core apples, discarding peeling and cores, and cube apple flesh directly into the juice mixture and stir frequently. Add up to another cup of water (total 2 cups) if needed, using only enough to provide a bath in which to begin cooling the apples. Place apples and juice bath in a pan and cook until apples are soft. Force cooked apples through a food mill or cone strainer (do not use a blender or food processor as this destroys the apple texture producing a product of less desirable consistency). Measure the resulting apple pulp, then add ½ to ⅔ cup of sugar for each cup of apple pulp depending on sweetness desired. Mix in salt and spice mixture. Add this mixture to the reduced apple cider in a 5 to 6 quart pan. Stirring continuously, heat to boiling while spooning off foam as it forms. When foam formation subsides, set burner control so apple butter cooks at a constant, gentle boil. Stirring occasionally, continue boiling uncovered for 20 to 25 minutes and remove any additional foam. Place a clean, small plate or saucer in the freezer to use to test apple butter. Apple butter is finished when about half a teaspoon, chilled on the cold plate, forms a soft gel. Ladle finished, hot apple butter into sterilized jars, filling to the brim. Clean any sticky; residue away from threaded tops of jars to allow a good seal. Cap immediately and screw lids on tight. Wipe jars clean and invert on a rack to cool.

Yield: 8 to 10 half pint jars of apple butter

Salads

Salads and Dressings

Ray Matthews

Onward and Upward in the Garden

"Gardening is an instrument of grace"
—MARY SARTON

Gardening has become an unexpected instrument of grace. Hours of inner peace can be obtained on one's knees, digging in the dirt among the vegetables. The sacrament of the moment when planting or weeding brings exquisite contentment. The mind is stilled and the heart expands. The Great Creator must have intended for us to flourish in a garden. And, when you pluck those first red-ripe tomatoes, the fine yellow squash, the green, firm cucumbers that grew in the soil you so tenderly tilled with sweaty brow and dirty fingernails, you will know that the adventures in the garden are a trajectory of forward motion, an evolution of soul.

New Potato and Asparagus Salad

3-4	pounds small new red potatoes	1	tablespoon lemon juice
	water	1-2	tablespoons olive oil
1	pound asparagus	2	tablespoons fresh chives, minced
1	tablespoon Dijon mustard		salt and fresh ground pepper, to taste

Clean and cut new potatoes in half. Cook in enough water to cover potatoes until tender, about 20 minutes. Drain and cool potatoes. Steam asparagus until crisp-tender, about 8 minutes, then plunge into cold water and drain. Cut asparagus into ½ inch pieces. Toss asparagus and potatoes gently together in a large bowl. In a separate small bowl, combine mustard, lemon juice and gradually whisk in olive oil. Pour over vegetables, add chives and season. Serve either cold or at room temperature.

Yield: 4 to 6 servings

Vegetable Medley Salad

1	(15 ounce) can French green beans	1	cup celery, chopped
1	(15 ounce) can green peas	1	onion, chopped
1	(15 ounce) can small kernel white corn	1	green bell pepper, chopped
1	(15 ounce) can lima beans	1	cup white vinegar
1	small jar (4 ounces) pimiento	1	cup sugar
		½	cup oil
			salt and pepper, optional and to taste

A favorite dish for all outdoor picnics.

Drain all canned vegetables and combine in large bowl with pimiento and chopped vegetables. In a blender, combine and blend well the vinegar, sugar, oil and salt and pepper, if used. Pour blender mix over all vegetables and toss. Refrigerate overnight. Pour off excess liquid before serving. May serve cold or at room temperature.

Yield: 14 servings

Broccoli Salad

3	cups fresh broccoli, chopped	3	slices bacon, cooked and crumbled
½	cup sunflower seeds	¼	cup sugar
½	cup white raisins	½	cup red wine vinegar
1	small red onion sliced into thin rings	¼	cup mayonnaise, low fat

Place first five ingredients in a bowl. Place the sugar, vinegar and mayonnaise in a tightly covered jar or container and shake vigorously until well blended. Pour over ingredients in the bowl and serve immediately.

Add a half cup grated sharp cheese for more zing, or vary the proportions of sugar, vinegar and mayonnaise to change tartness, sweetness and creaminess of the dressing according to your own taste.

Yield: 4 servings

Festive Fresh Spinach with Vinaigrette Dressing

2	tablespoons balsamic vinegar	1	bunch fresh spinach, torn
2	tablespoons light olive oil	¼	cup toasted almonds
2	tablespoons water	¼	cup raisins
2	tablespoons sugar	1	small apple, cored and diced
2	tablespoons onion, minced	1	can mandarin oranges (small or large size can as dictated by your taste)
½	teaspoon salt		
½	teaspoon curry		

Mix first seven ingredients (vinegar through curry) together. Place spinach, almonds and fruits in a salad bowl. Pour dressing over the items in the salad bowl to coat with dressing.

It's the curry that really makes this recipe work.

Yield: 6 to 8 servings

A Celtic Prayer
Bless the fruits of the earth.
Bless the hands of the farmers.
Bless the calloused hands of migrant workers.
Bless the texture and the colors of my food.
Bless the creativity of the cooks.
Bless the flavors and pleasing aroma of my food.
Bless all who share bread with the hungry poor.
Bless those who gather.
Bless the breaking of the bread.
Blessed Be!
Blessed Be!
Blessed Be!
Christ at every table.
Christ beside me,
Christ behind me,
Christ around me,
In the breaking of the bread.

Asparagus Vinaigrette

2	pounds fresh asparagus		salt and pepper, to taste
	water, salted	¼	cup olive oil
¼	cup chopped pimiento	2	tablespoons balsamic
3	tablespoons shallots or		vinegar
	scallions, chopped		

Wash asparagus and remove tough lower ends of stalks. Cook asparagus in boiling, salted water with cover ajar until tender but not mushy; about 5 minutes (keeping lid ajar allows acids to escape with steam and allows asparagus to retain its dark green color). Drain asparagus and immediately plunge stalks into ice water to stop further cooking. Roll asparagus gently in a clean towel to remove excess water. Place one third of the asparagus in a shallow serving dish. Top with ⅓ the pimiento and shallots or scallions and sprinkle with salt and pepper. Repeat to make three layers. Pour oil and vinegar over top. Gently turn asparagus to distribute seasonings throughout. Cover and chill at least 2 hours before serving.

Yield: 6 to 8 servings

Mimi Iacone likes to use any leftovers from this dish as a flavorful addition to any tossed salad or cooked into scrambled eggs and topped with Parmesan cheese. Problem is there are seldom any leftovers to use.

Poppy Seed Fruit Salad

2	(11 ounce) cans mandarin oranges, drained	1	(10 ounce) package frozen strawberries, thawed
1	(16 ounce) can peach slices, drained	1	(3½ ounce) package instant vanilla pudding mix
2	(15 ounce) cans pineapple chunks, drained	1	cup orange juice
4	bananas, sliced	1	teaspoon poppy seeds

Place fruit (the first five ingredients) in large salad bowl. In another bowl, mix the pudding, orange juice and poppy seeds. Pour over fruit

Yield: 12 servings

Mary Bobbitt advises that you may add any other fresh fruit in season and increase thereby the number of servings. She says this salad is great with ham or chicken, to take to sick friends or serve on any occasion. It keeps well for several days when refrigerated.

Salads

Frozen Southern Cream Cheese Salad

2 (3 ounce) packages cream cheese
4 tablespoons mayonnaise
1 teaspoon lemon juice
1 teaspoon Maraschino cherry juice
1 tablespoon pineapple juice
1 (8 ounce) can crushed pineapple, drained
1 cup miniature marshmallows
12 Maraschino cherries, chopped
½ cup chopped nuts

Blend first five ingredients together. Stir in remaining ingredients and mix well. Spread into a loaf pan and freeze. To serve, cut into 1 inch slices and place on a lettuce leaf for garnish. Allow to stand at room temperature for five to ten minutes before eating.

Yield: 8 servings

This was a favorite at home when growing up in the 1950's for Betsy Steketee. It was her job to make this salad on Saturday for Sunday dinner. She froze it in old-time aluminum ice cube trays; the ones with removable dividers.

Mango Salad

½ cup non-fat plain or vanilla yogurt
1 tablespoon prepared horseradish
1 tablespoon white vinegar
⅛ teaspoon pepper
1 cup strawberries
½ cup red bell pepper, chopped
2 cups mango, peeled and cubed

Combine first four ingredients in a medium bowl and whisk to mix. Set aside. Wash strawberries, remove and discard stems. Cut strawberries in half. Combine strawberries, bell pepper and mango in a medium bowl. Gently fold in enough of the yogurt dressing mixture to coat the bell pepper, mango and strawberries.

Yield: 4 to 6 servings

"I am the true vine, and my Father is the gardener. He cuts off every branch in me that bears no fruit, while every branch that does bear fruit he prunes so that it will be even more fruitful... I am the vine, you are the branches."

John 15: 1-2, and 5

Winter Fruit Salad

1	(28 ounce) can sliced peaches, drained	½	pound fresh seedless grapes, green or red
1	(28 ounce) can pears, drained and sliced	3	kiwi fruit, pealed and sliced
1	(11 ounce) can mandarin oranges, drained	1	(21 ounce) can peach pie filling
1	(16 ounce) bag frozen strawberries, thawed and quartered	2	fresh apples, cored and sliced (optional)

Mix all ingredients and chill for at least one hour.

Keeps refrigerated for several days.

Yield: 12 servings

Versatile Fresh Fruit Salad

	lemon juice, to taste	fresh minced gingerroot, to taste
2	tablespoons honey	
2	cups favorite fruit juice (apple, orange, etc.)	fresh seasonal fruit, enough for 3 to 4 cups cut up

Blend lemon juice, honey, and just enough fruit juice (about two cups or a little less) to make a smooth consistency. Add minced gingerroot to taste. Clean and immediately slice, cut or dice seasonal fruit directly into the juice mixture stirring frequently as fruit is added. Ensure juice coats each piece of fruit.

The juices coating the fruit prevent browning.

Yield: 6 to 8 servings or may vary with amount of fruit used

Tinka Martin uses mostly citrus fruits in winter and melons and berries in summer. Apples, bananas and grapes are good anytime. This dish is not only a salad, but also a good appetizer, side dish or dessert, compatible with everything. Tinka says "It is my covered-dish choice for all occasions."

Chicken Salad with Old Bay

2½	cups cooked chicken, cubed	2	teaspoons Old Bay seasoning
1	cup low-fat mayonnaise	4	stalks celery, diced
6	ounces ranch dressing	½	teaspoon salt
		½	teaspoon pepper

Mix all ingredients together and serve on lettuce leaf, in pita pocket or on bread.

Yield: 6 (4 ounce) servings

Aunt Jeanne's Favorite Antipasto

Dressing

½ cup vinegar

2½ teaspoons salt

¼ teaspoon pepper

2½ teaspoons oregano, or more to taste

1 clove garlic, minced

1 teaspoon thyme

¼ cup oil

Salad Body

salami, cubed

provolone cheese or other white cheese, cubed

artichokes, cubed

black pitted olives, whole or sliced

green and/or red bell peppers, ¼ inch slices or rings or diced coarsely

celery, diced coarsely

Mix dressing ingredients putting oil in last. For salad body, amount of ingredients depends on how many servings desired, and how large each is cubed or coarsely diced. Marinate salad body in the dressing overnight.

This dish can be an appetizer if meats are cut in larger pieces.

Yield: ¾ cup dressing, amount of salad is variable

Simply Macaroni Salad

8	ounces elbow macaroni, cooked using package directions and drained
4	eggs, hard-boiled and chopped
½	green bell pepper, chopped
4	stalks celery, chopped
1	small onion, chopped
½	pound sharp cheddar cheese, shredded
1	pint mayonnaise
	salt, to taste
	Parmesan cheese, grated

Combine all ingredients except Parmesan cheese. Sprinkle this on top just before serving.

Yield: 8 servings

The ritual is One. The food is One. We who offer the food are One. The fire of hunger is also One. All action is One. We who understand this are One.

Ancient Hindu Grace.

Vegetable Aspic Ring

3	envelopes unflavored gelatin (such as Knox)
12	ounces V-8 juice
1	(28 ounce) can stewed tomatoes, undrained
¼	cup lemon juice
4	teaspoons Worcestershire sauce
1	teaspoon salt
	hot sauce, dash
2	(15 ounce) cans or jars three bean salad, drained
¾	cup green onion, finely chopped
	Bibb lettuce, to garnish
	mayonnaise, optional

Soften gelatin in V-8 juice. In a saucepan, bring tomatoes to a boil, stir in gelatin mixture and heat until gelatin dissolves. Stir in lemon juice, Worcestershire sauce, salt and hot sauce. Add the three bean salad and onion. Pour into a lightly oiled 8 cup gelatin mold and chill until firm. Unmold on a bed of bibb lettuce and serve with mayonnaise dollop on top, if desired.

Yield: 10 to 12 servings

Health Salad

1 (3 ounce) package lemon
   gelatin
1 cup water
1 (20 ounce) can crushed
   pineapple with juice
1 cup (or more) carrots,
   grated

salt pinch
lettuce leaves, optional
   garnish
mayonnaise, optional
   garnish

Dissolve gelatin in boiling water in a 9 x 9 inch dish. Add pineapple, pineapple juice, carrots and salt. Mix and refrigerate to set. Serve on a lettuce leaf with mayonnaise garnish.

Yield: 4 to 6 servings

Lime Veggie Salad

3 (3 ounce) packages lime
   gelatin
3 cups hot water
1 large cucumber, grated
1 medium onion, grated

1 cup celery, finely
   chopped
1 teaspoon salt
4 tablespoons vinegar

Dissolve gelatin in hot water in a 9 x 12 inch dish. Add celery. Mix. Add salt and vinegar. Mix. Add cucumber and onions. Mix. Chill until set.

Yield: 9 to 12 servings

Marylou Hogan's father's favorite when served warm with crumbled bacon on lettuce, spinach, or asparagus.

Boiled Salad Dressing

3 eggs
1 cup sugar

½ cup cider vinegar
½ cup water

In a saucepan, beat eggs and then add sugar. Stir. Add vinegar and water. Bring mixture to a boil while stirring constantly (if too thick, add more water up to another ½ cup). Cool and store in a clean jar with a tight lid.

Yield: 1½ cups

Bleu Cheese Dressing

¾	cup sour cream	1	teaspoon Worcestershire sauce
½	teaspoon dry mustard		
½	teaspoon ground black pepper	1⅓	cups mayonnaise
¼	teaspoon salt	4	ounces imported Danish bleu cheese, crumbled
¼-½	teaspoon garlic		

Place first six item in a mixing bowl and blend with beaters 2 minutes on low speed. Add mayonnaise and blend another 30 seconds on low speed. Blend on medium speed for 2 minutes. Add cheese and blend at low speed for minimum 3 minutes and absolute maximum of 4 minutes and no longer. Refrigerate and let set 24 hours before using.

Yield: 2½ cups

Cole Slaw Dressing

1	cup sugar	1	teaspoon salt
1	cup vinegar	¼	cup onion, chopped
1	teaspoon celery seed	¼	cup green or red bell pepper, chopped
1	teaspoon mustard seed		

Heat the sugar and vinegar slowly to dissolve sugar. Do not boil. Remove from heat and add remaining ingredients. Store refrigerated in clean jar with tight cover. Add to shredded cabbage at least 4 hours before serving.

Sweet pickle relish may be substituted for the bell pepper.

Stores for over a year if kept in a sterilized jar well covered.

Yield: 2½ cups

Lemon Vinaigrette Dressing

1	quart olive oil	1	teaspoon oregano
1	pint vinegar	1	teaspoon dry basil
½	cup water	¼	cup sugar
1	clove fresh garlic, chopped	1	teaspoon salt
1	teaspoon onion, minced	¼	cup lemon juice

Mix all ingredients in a shaker and pour.

Yield: 7 cups

Cool Cucumber Dressing

1	cup cucumbers, finely chopped	¼	cup plain yogurt
1	clove garlic, finely chopped	¼	cup low-calorie mayonnaise
½	cup green pepper, chopped	¼	cup chili sauce
½	teaspoon salt	1	tablespoon prepared mustard

Combine all ingredients and let set refrigerated, covered, overnight.

Yield: 12 servings

Side Dishes

Vegetables, Pickles and Relishes, Sauces and Marinades

Ann Hines

The Celebration Table

*"I learned early on that setting a table is so much
more than just laying down knives and forks.
It is creating a setting for food and conversation,
setting a mood and an aura that lingers long after
what was served and who said what was forgotten."*
—PERI WOLFMAN

When preparing a table, we want our guests to appreciate the way the table looks. After we have set out the china, stemware, and linens, we step back and try to envision what it will look like with the food all laid out in picture-perfect order. It would be hard to imagine a beautiful table without all those little extras: the salad, soup, and relishes. These colorful and delicious condiments are like bouquets of summer flowers. They elevate eating into the exquisite pleasure of dining. Gardens and farmers' markets now enable us to serve fresh salads, homemade soups and relishes all year round. The simple pleasure of watching our guests enjoy a delicious green salad laced with edible flowers or spooning a rich chutney on a thick slice of ham can be a continual feast at Mother Nature's table.

Twice Baked Potatoes

4	medium to large russet potatoes, scrubbed	¼	cup favorite cheese (recommend grated cheddar or cream cheese)
4	strips bacon, cooked crisp and chopped		
¼	cup milk	2	tablespoons chives, chopped
2	tablespoons sour cream		salt and pepper, to taste

Preheat oven to 350 degrees. Place clean potatoes evenly spread on middle rack in oven and bake until tender to touch, about 60 to 75 minutes. Remove potatoes, leaving oven on, and let potatoes cool 3 minutes or until easy to handle. Cut potatoes in half, lengthwise. Spoon out insides leaving enough potato in the skin as a definite shell for stuffing. Lightly oil each shell and place on aluminum foil covered pan. Place shells in oven for 10 minutes (this adds firmness and crispness to the overall dish). While this is being done, combine the scooped out potato with all other ingredients using a fork to mix well and mash together. To keep mashed mix warm until shells are ready, spoon the mixture into a plastic bag and wrap bag in aluminum foil. Remove shells from oven, turn oven to broil, and spoon potato mixture into shells, distributing evenly. Place pan with stuffed shells in oven for 5 to 10 minutes until lightly browned.

Yield: 8 servings

Mashed Potato Casserole

1½ pounds russet potatoes (about 5 potatoes), peeled and cut into 2 inch cubes

water, lightly salted

6 cups shredded green cabbage (about one small head)

4 ounces reduced-fat cream cheese, softened and cut into pieces

1 teaspoon salt

½ cup scallions, thinly sliced

freshly ground black pepper, to taste

1 cup extra-sharp cheddar cheese, grated

Preheat oven to 425 degrees. In another pan, steam shredded cabbage for about 6 minutes. In another pan, boil potato cubes in lightly salted water until soft enough to mash, about 20 minutes. Drain potatoes, return them to pan and place on low heat and shake for about 30 seconds to remove excess moisture. Remove from heat and mash potatoes. Add cream cheese, salt and mix. Fold in scallions and steamed cabbage. Pepper to taste. Spread mixture into a lightly oiled 3 quart baking dish and top with grated cheese. Bake uncovered at 425 degrees for 30 to 50 minutes. Let stand 10 minutes before serving.

Yield: 12 servings

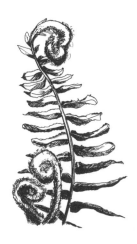

Red Cabbage, German Style

3 tablespoons butter or margarine	⅓ cup white vinegar
3 Granny Smith apples, sliced thin	½ cup brown sugar, firmly packed
1 small onion, chopped	2 teaspoons all-purpose flour
1 small red cabbage (about 1¾ pounds), shredded	1 teaspoon salt
	¼ teaspoon pepper
	⅓ cup dry red wine

Melt butter in a large skillet over medium-high heat. Add apples and onion and sauté 5 minutes. Add cabbage and vinegar. In a bowl, stir together sugar, flour, salt and pepper; sprinkle over cabbage. Add wine, cover and reduce heat to simmer. Simmer while stirring often for 35 minutes.

Yield: 6 servings

Curried Baked Cauliflower

1 large head cauliflower	4 ounces cheddar cheese, shredded
½ teaspoon salt	½ cup mayonnaise
water	1 teaspoon curry powder
1 (10½ ounce) can cream of chicken soup	2 tablespoons butter
	¼ cup bread crumbs

Preheat oven to 350 degrees. Cut cauliflower into large serving pieces. Boil in salted water until "crunchy." Drain. Place cooked cauliflower in a lightly buttered casserole dish. In a bowl, mix the soup, cheese, mayonnaise and curry. Pour over cauliflower. Melt 2 tablespoons butter in a saucepan. Add breadcrumbs to the melted butter and sprinkle mixture over cauliflower. Bake at 350 degrees for 30 minutes.

Yield: 6 servings

"Friendship"
by Dinah
M. M. Craik
Oh, the comfort —
the inexpressible
comfort of feeling
safe with a person,
Having neither to
weigh thoughts,
Nor measure words
— but pouring them
All right out —
just as they are —
Chaff and grain
together —
Certain that a
faithful hand will
Take and sift
them —
Keep what is
worth keeping —
And with the
breath of kindness
Blow the rest away.

Broccoli or Veg-All Casserole

20 ounces frozen chopped broccoli or broccoli florets, or 2 (15 ounce) cans Veg-All, drained

2 eggs, beaten

1 cup cream of celery soup

1 small onion, chopped fine

1 cup sharp cheddar cheese, grated

1 cup mayonnaise

1 cup (or more) Ritz crackers, crumbled

4 tablespoons butter, melted

Submitted by two cooks, Julie Layfield and Judy Boatwright, they claim this recipe is fantastic for getting the stubborn to eat broccoli or mixed vegetables.

Preheat oven to 350 degrees. Cook broccoli, if used, 5 minutes according to package directions. Drain. Mix broccoli or Veg-All with all other ingredients except crackers and melted butter. In a 7½ x 11 inch casserole dish, lightly greased, pour in vegetable mixture, sprinkle top with cracker crumbs, and then pour melted butter over crumbs. Bake at 350 degrees for 30 minutes.

For a low fat dish, use egg beaters, reduced fat soup, low-fat cheese and low-fat mayonnaise.

Yield: 6 to 8 servings

Asparagus and Pasta

1 pound (or 1½ pounds) fresh asparagus

3 cups pasta (about a ½ pound)

½ cup heavy cream

2 tablespoons butter

½ cup Parmesan cheese, grated

Wash asparagus carefully to remove all "grit" and cut into 1 inch piece. Steam 5 minutes. Cook pasta as directed by package and drain. Combine cream and butter in a saucepan and boil 3 minutes. Combine asparagus, pasta and cream and ¼ cup of the grated cheese and heat all ingredients through. Place in serving bowl or directly onto dinner plates and sprinkle top with the remaining cheese.

Yield: 2 to 3 servings

Broccoli Rice Casserole

1 tablespoon butter	1 (10¾ ounce) can condensed cream of mushroom soup, undiluted
1 small onion, chopped fine	
½ cup celery, chopped fine	
1 (10 ounce) package frozen chopped broccoli, thawed	1 (5 ounce) can evaporated milk
	3 cups cooked rice
1 (8 ounce) jar cheese spread	

Preheat oven to 325 degrees. In a large skillet over medium heat, sauté the butter, onion, celery, and broccoli for 3 to 5 minutes. In a bowl, stir together cheese, soup, and milk until smooth. In a lightly greased 8 inch casserole dish, place rice. And then layer on top evenly the vegetable mixture. Pour cheese mixture over all. Bake at 325 degrees for 25 to 30 minutes until hot and bubbly.

Yield: 8 to 10 servings

This recipe is offered in memory of Marilyn O'Bleness' sister, Lucille Honeycutt. This was her recipe which she submitted to her church's cookbook project just prior to her death.

Cold Marinated Carrots

2 pounds carrots, cut into bite-size pieces	½ cup cooking oil
	½ cup vinegar
½ medium onion, chopped	1 tablespoon Worcestershire sauce
1 green bell pepper, chopped	
	¼ teaspoon dry mustard
1 cup tomato soup	1 teaspoon salt
¾ cup sugar	

Mix all ingredients together and refrigerate for 24 hours. Serve cold.

Yield: 8 servings

Judy Boatwright says this is a "must" dish for all carrot haters. "Even my children will eat this one."

Zesty Carrots

8	medium carrots, diced	1	teaspoon salt
½	cup mayonnaise	¼	teaspoon pepper
2	tablespoons onion, grated		bread crumbs
2	tablespoons horseradish		butter

While this cookbook was being developed, a great many people wanted to be reassured that this Rev. Charles E. B. Gill's recipe was definitely going to be included.

Preheat oven to 350 degrees. Cook carrots in a small amount of water until tender. Drain. Combine all ingredients except bread crumbs in a lightly buttered casserole dish and top with bread crumbs as desirable. Dot with butter as desired. Bake 15 minutes at 350 degrees.

May be made up ahead of time and baked just before serving.

Yield: 8 servings

Microwave Baked Vidalia Onions

4	large Vidalia onions	4	tablespoons butter or margarine
	Coarse black pepper, to taste		Parmesan cheese, grated

Peel and core each onion. Be sure you core them ALMOST through but not completely; to the bottom. Lightly grease a microwave dish and place onions in dish. Sprinkle pepper into cored center and then place one tablespoon butter or margarine into core. Sprinkle generously with Parmesan cheese. Cover dish and microwave until soft, about 15 to 20 minutes.

Great dish for onion lovers and one to experiment with other herbs and cheeses.

Yield: 4 servings

Cherry Tomato Gratin

¼ cup plain bread crumbs
¼ cup Parmesan cheese,
    grated
1 tablespoon olive oil
¼ teaspoon black pepper

1 clove garlic, crushed
2 pints cherry tomatoes
2 tablespoons fresh
    parsley, chopped

Preheat oven to 425 degrees. In a small bowl combine bread crumbs, cheese, oil, pepper and garlic. Wash tomatoes and place in a shallow 1½ quart casserole dish or a 9½ inch Pyrex pie dish. Top with bread crumb mixture and sprinkle with parsley. Bake at 425 degrees until tomatoes are heated through and crumbs are browned, about 20 minutes.

Yield: 6 servings

Great recipe when you have a lot of cherry tomatoes and don't know what to do with them. Here's an answer from Mike and Cammie Walker.

Stuffed Tomatoes

6 medium to large ripe
    tomatoes
½ cup butter

2 tablespoons brown
    sugar
3 ounces seasoned
    croutons, crushed

Preheat oven to 325 degrees. Wash tomatoes and cut out stem leaving a small hole in top. Scoop out pulp by way of the small top hole. In a saucepan melt the butter and mix in the brown sugar and crushed croutons. Stuff tomatoes with this filling and arrange tomatoes in a baking dish. Bake at 325 degrees for 20 to 30 minutes. Serve warm.

This is a delicious, easy summertime side dish to serve with grilled fish or chicken

Yield: 6 servings

Squash and Carrot Creamy Casserole

2	pounds fresh yellow squash (or 2 10-ounce packages frozen squash)	1	small onion, grated
		½	pint sour cream
		½	cup margarine or butter, melted
1	tablespoon diced pimiento	1	(16 ounce) package Pepperidge Farm herb dressing
1	large carrot, grated		
1	(10½ ounce) can cream of chicken soup		

Preheat oven to 350 degrees. If using fresh squash, wash and slice before cooking. Cook squash until tender. Drain. If using frozen squash, cook as directed by package until tender. Add remaining ingredients except for margarine and herb dressing. Mix thoroughly, but do not beat. In a separate bowl, melt margarine and mix with herb dressing. Divide the moistened dressing in half. Press one half into the bottom of a lightly buttered 8 to 9 inch casserole dish. Add vegetable mixture. Spoon and "spread" remaining half of dressing over top. Bake at 350 degrees until golden brown on top, about 45 minutes.

Yield: 8 servings

Italian Spinach Topped Tomatoes

1	cup water	1	(9 ounce) package frozen chopped spinach, thawed and well drained
2	tablespoons butter		
½	teaspoon salt		
¼-½	teaspoon oregano	1-2	medium tomatoes cut into 6 slices each (slices about ¼ inch thick)
1½	cups instant mashed potato flakes		
½	cup milk		
1	egg		Parmesan cheese, grated fresh or canned, to taste

In a medium saucepan, combine water, butter, salt and oregano. Bring to a boil, remove from heat and immediately add potato flakes, milk and egg. Mix well with fork. Gradually fold drained spinach into this mixture. In an ungreased 9 x 13 inch pan, place the tomatoes in a single layer, mound ½ cup of the potato and spinach mixture on top of each tomato slice and sprinkle generously with cheese in an amount desired. Broil (or bake at moderate temperature, about 275 to 325 degrees) until cheese is slightly brown, watching closely to avoid burning.

Looks very pretty and tastes great.

Yield: 4 to 6 servings

Above all, love each other deeply, because love covers over a multitude of sins. Offer hospitality to one another without grumbling. Each one should use whatever gift he has received to serve others, faithfully administering God's grace in its various forms.

1 Peter 4: 8-10

Tomato and Broccoli Bake

4   ounces macaroni (about
    1 cup uncooked)
2   cups broccoli, chopped
1   small onion, diced
2   tablespoons butter
    minced garlic, to taste
    (about ½ teaspoon)
    oregano, to taste (about
    ½ teaspoon)

basil, to taste (about ½
teaspoon dried oregano
but use fresh if possible)
5   tomatoes, peeled and
    cored, then diced
1   cup fresh parsley,
    chopped
¼   cup chicken broth
1   cup cheddar cheese,
    shredded

Preheat oven to 375 degrees. Cook pasta as directed by package. Partially cook broccoli. Sauté onion in butter. Combine all other ingredients except pasta, broccoli, and cheese in a saucepan. Bring to a boil. Reduce heat and simmer covered for 4 minutes. Add pasta and broccoli, mix and spread mixture in a baking dish. Cover and bake at 375 degrees for 15 minutes. Uncover, sprinkle cheese on top and cook uncovered an additional 5 minutes.

Yield: 2 to 3 servings

Grama Shimer's Baked Beans

This recipe is easy to double and easy to vary the ingredients to suit to taste, such as more onion, less sugar, etc. David Brassington and his mother say, though, to never use anything but Furman's brand white beans. Seldom are there any leftovers.

2   (about 14½ ounces
    each) cans Furman's
    white beans
8   ounces tomato sauce or
    stewed tomatoes
½   cup dark molasses

1   medium onion, scored or
    coarsely diced
½   cup dark brown sugar
½   cup water
¼   teaspoon cumin
¼   pound bacon

Preheat oven to 350 degrees. Combine all ingredients in a bean pot or casserole dish. Cook uncovered in oven for about one hour, stirring now and again. Cover after one hour and continue to cook at reduced heat (200 to 220 degrees) for an additional 4 to 5 hours. Stir and add more water as needed to keep casserole moist and prevent burning.

Yield: 6 to 8 servings

Vegetarian Black Bean Casserole

cooking oil spray
1 tablespoon olive oil
1 medium onion, chopped
½ cup green bell pepper, chopped
2 cloves garlic, chopped
2 (15½ ounce) cans black beans with juice
1½ cups tomato salsa

1 teaspoon oregano
⅓ cup chopped cilantro (same as coriander or Chinese parsley)
8 corn tortillas
1 10 ounce package frozen white corn, thawed and drained
2 cups Monterey Jack cheese with jalapeños, grated

Preheat oven to 400 degrees. Spray a 9 x 12 inch baking dish with cooling oil. In a skillet, sauté onion, pepper and garlic. Mix into a bowl with black beans and salsa. Add seasonings. Spread ⅓ of this mixture in the baking dish, top with 4 corn tortillas. Spread a second layer of ⅓ the bean and salsa mixture, then a layer of ½ the package of corn, then ½ the cheese, and then the remaining tortillas. Top with remaining ⅓ of bean and salsa mixture, then the second ½ of the corn, and then the second ½ of the cheese. Cover with foil and bake for 20 minutes at 400 degrees. Remove foil and continue to bake an added 10 minutes uncovered. Let stand 10 minutes before serving.

Yield: 6 servings

Now that I am about to eat, O Great Spirit, give my thanks to the beasts and birds whom You have provided for my hunger, and pray deliver my sorrow that living things must make a sacrifice for my comfort and well being. Let the feather of corn spring up in its time and let it not wither but make full grain for the fires of our cooking pots, now that I am about to eat.

Native American Grace, New Mexico.

Pig Roasted Beans

1-2	tablespoons bacon drippings or olive oil	1	(32 ounce) can tomatoes
1	large cooking apple, chopped	1	cup brown sugar
½	cup onion, chopped	1½	tablespoons curry powder
1	large green bell pepper, chopped		Parmesan cheese, canned dry or fresh, to taste
2	(16 ounce) cans light kidney beans		

Preheat oven to 350 degrees. Sauté apple, onion and pepper in bacon drippings or olive oil. Drain beans and tomatoes well. Mix all ingredients except Parmesan cheese and place in an uncovered 2 quart casserole at 350 degrees for about 20 to 25 minutes. Top generously with Parmesan cheese and continue baking for another 5 to 10 minutes.

This dish freezes well.

Yield: 6 to 8 servings

The bread is pure and fresh. The water is cool and clear. Lord of all life, be with us. Lord of all life, be near.

African Grace.

Pineapple Soufflé

½	cup butter, softened	5	slices white bread, crusts removed and discarded and bread cubed
1	cup sugar		
4	eggs		
1	(8 ounce) can crushed pineapple, drained		

Preheat oven to 350 degrees. Cream together the butter and sugar. Add eggs one at a time. Stir well with each egg added. Stir in drained pineapple. Add bread and mix until bread is moist but not mushy. Pour into greased 2 quart casserole dish. Bake at 350 degrees for about 1 hour.

Yield: 6 servings

Grandmother's Bread and Butter Pickles

6	quarts medium cucumbers, sliced	6	cups sugar
6	medium onions, sliced thin	½	cup mustard seed
1	cup salt	1	tablespoon celery seed
1½	quarts vinegar	⅓	teaspoon cayenne pepper

Combine cucumbers, onions and salt and let stand for three hours. Drain, reserving cucumber and onions. Do not rinse. In a large pot, combine vinegar with remaining ingredients and bring to a boil. Add reserved cucumbers and onions. Heat to simmering, being careful to avoid boiling. Once pot begins to simmer, immediately remove from heat and quickly pack into sterile jars and seal at once.

Yield: 12 quarts

Molasses Apple Chutney

1	(20 ounce) can apple slices or equivalent prepared at home	½	cup vinegar
		½	teaspoon salt
½	cup raisins	1	teaspoon ground ginger
¾	cup dark molasses	1	teaspoon dry mustard
		1	teaspoon curry powder

Combine all ingredients in a saucepan. Bring to a boil, stirring occasionally. Reduce heat and simmer for 15 minutes. Serve hot or cold as a meat accompaniment.

Great with almost any meat and makes a great gift as well.

Yield: 3 cups

At this table be our Host, Father, Son and Holy Ghost; Food and drink are from above, Tokens of Your heavenly love.
Amen.

Green Tomato Relish

6	pounds green tomatoes	3	tablespoons salt
2-3	medium onions	1½	teaspoons celery seed
2	medium red bell peppers	½	teaspoon cinnamon
1	medium green bell pepper	½	teaspoon ground cloves
1	large stalk celery	½	teaspoon ground allspice
2	cups distilled white vinegar	½	teaspoon ground turmeric
1⅔	cups granulated sugar	¼	teaspoon cayenne pepper

Wash, trim and quarter all vegetables. Put through food processor. Drain and discard liquid. Combine vinegar, sugar, salt and spices in a saucepan and bring to a boil. Add drained vegetables, reduce heat and simmer for 10 minutes, stirring occasionally. Pack one clean pint jar at a time, filling to within ½ inch of top and making sure vinegar liquid covers the vegetables. Cap at once. Process (immerse up to the jar's neck) all jars for 5 minutes in boiling water bath.

Yield: 5 to 6 pints

Brandied Cranberries

3	cups fresh cranberries	⅓	cup brandy
1½	cups sugar		

This is Shirley Barrett's favorite way to do cranberries and just what the doctor ordered.

Preheat oven to 300 degrees. Combine all ingredients in a large bowl. Stir well. Spoon mixture into a 13 x 9 x 2 inch baking dish. Cover and bake at 300 degrees for 1 hour. Remove from oven. Serve warm or cold with poultry or pork.

Yield: 2 cups

Kiwi-Onion Chutney

1 cup vinegar	½ cup onion, sliced thinly
1 cup brown sugar	½ cup lemon, unpeeled
¾ teaspoon salt	and sliced thinly
½ teaspoon ground ginger	½ cup raisins
⅛ teaspoon red pepper	1½ cup kiwi, peeled and
1 cup apples, cored,	chopped
peeled and chopped	

Heat vinegar, sugar, salt, ginger and pepper on medium to the point of simmering. Do not boil. Add apple, onion, lemon and raisins, cooking at a simmer for 10 minutes. Add kiwi and increase heat. Bring to a boil, remove from heat at once and allow to cool. Take ¾ cup of this mixture and place in blender. Blend until smooth. Return to remainder of mixture. Chill. Keep refrigerated until used.

Excellent when served with creamed cheese or yogurt and crackers.

Yield: 3 to 4 cups

Marinara Sauce

¼ cup extra-virgin olive oil	¼ cup parsley, coarsely chopped
4 cloves garlic, chopped	2 tablespoons basil
1 (28 ounce) can plum tomatoes, coarsely chopped	2 tablespoons oregano
	salt and pepper, to taste

Heat oil in a large heavy pot over medium heat. Add garlic and sauté until slightly brown but not burned, about 3 to 4 minutes. Remove from heat and stir in tomatoes. Return the pot to medium heat and simmer uncovered 30 minutes. Add remaining ingredients and simmer another 15 minutes. Cool and refrigerate overnight before serving over linguine.

Yield: 4 servings

Pesto Sauce

2	cups fresh basil, packed firm
2	large garlic cloves, minced

½	cup pine nuts
¾	cup fresh Parmesan cheese, grated
⅔	cup olive oil

Blend all ingredients to form a sauce for use on pasta.

Freeze in an ice cube tray for future use. When frozen, separate from tray and store in freezer bags in freezer. Use one cube per serving.

Yield: 4 cups

Let your conversation be always full of grace, seasoned with salt, so that you may know how to answer everyone.

Colossians 4: 6.

Governor Sauce

2	quarts ripe tomatoes
2	quarts green tomatoes
1	large head of cabbage
12	medium onions
3	red bell peppers
1	cup salt

2	quarts cider vinegar
1½	pounds sugar (3¼ cups)
½	cup yellow mustard seed
1	tablespoon celery seed

Chop or grind all vegetables fine. Salt overnight. Mix well, drain. Rinse thoroughly and drain again. Add vinegar, sugar and seeds. Put in large pot and heat to boiling. Boil for 30 minutes. Can mixture in jars using a heat seal process.

Yield: 6 quarts

Black Bean Salsa

⅓ cup red wine vinegar

⅓ cup olive oil

½ teaspoon ground black pepper

3 cloves garlic, finely minced

3 (15-16 ounce) cans black beans, drained and rinsed and drained again

1 large green bell pepper, chopped

1 large red bell pepper, chopped

1 large purple onion, chopped

2 (15-16 ounce) cans diced fresh cut tomatoes, Mexican style, drained

2 small cans (4.5 ounces each) chopped green chilies, drained

1 (10 ounce) package frozen niblet corn

Combine first four ingredients and let stand while preparing remaining ingredients. Rinse and drain beans. Chop peppers and onion, and dice, if needed, tomatoes and chilies. In a bowl, pour the first four ingredient mixture over the vegetables and mix gently. Refrigerate overnight before serving with taco chips.

Yield: 12½ cups

Glory to you for the feast-day of life.
Glory to you for the perfume of lilies and roses.
Glory to you for each different taste of berry and fruit.
Glory to you for the sparkling silver of early morning dew.
Glory to you for the joy of dawn's awakening.
Glory to you for the new life each day brings.

Gregory Petrov.

Amigo's Chili Sauce

18	tomatoes	1	teaspoon salt
3	green bell peppers	1	teaspoons allspice
2	medium onions	½	teaspoon ground cloves
3	tiny hot peppers, seeded	½	teaspoon ground cinnamon
2	cups vinegar		
1	cup sugar		

This particular recipe came from Mike Walker's mother. Cammie, Mike's wife, says it's wonderful as a relish or sauce for ham.

Skin tomatoes by placing in a large pot and pouring boiling water in to cover them. Drain after 3 to 4 minutes and set aside. Dice or coarsely grind, independently, the green peppers, onions and hot peppers. Last, dice or coarsely grind the tomatoes as this is very messy. Return tomatoes to the pot and add the prepared peppers and onions. Add all remaining ingredients. Cook slowly over low to medium heat until thick, approximately 2 hours.

Yield: 3 pints

Agnes' Mother's Special Marinade Sauce

1	(12 ounce) jar soy sauce	¼	cup crushed red pepper powder (available at Asian groceries)
10	(or more) cloves garlic, peeled and flattened	1	bunch scallions, chopped (discard top greens)
¼	cup roasted sesame seeds	1	tablespoon sugar
		1	teaspoon sesame oil

Mix all ingredients together and store in refrigerator for at least two days.

Versatile and keeps in refrigerator about three months. Great when used as marinade for chicken, pork, beef or tofu. Also goes well in stir fried vegetable dishes or mixed with rice.

Yield: 1½ cups

Roast Rub

2 tablespoons Greek Cavender's seasoning (found in any store's spice section)	1 tablespoon Accent seasoning
	1 tablespoon pepper
	1 tablespoon salt
	4 tablespoons soy sauce

Mix all dry ingredients. Add soy sauce, one tablespoon at a time, and mix thoroughly until it becomes a thick paste. Rub completely and lavishly into all sides of venison, beef or pork roast. Wrap roast tightly in tin foil. Roast, bake or grill as desired.

Yield: 1 large roast (about 8 servings)

Stan White says that this rub is guaranteed to make the toughest meat tender.

Terry's Baste for Grilled Fish

honey, to taste	lemon juice, to taste
horseradish, to taste	

Mix ingredients to suit your taste. Place favorite fish fillets in a grilling basket for fish and place over hot coals. Baste lavishly while cooking.

Yield: as much as you want to make

This recipe was acquired by Sarah Spink Downing in an exchange on the end of the Outer Banks Pier. What better place to find a great and easy fish baste recipe?

Horseradish

Sour Cream Sauce for Vegetables

4 teaspoons light brown sugar	1 teaspoon Worcestershire sauce
¼ teaspoon dry mustard	¼ teaspoon salt
2½ teaspoons vinegar	¼ teaspoon pepper
	⅓ cup dairy sour cream

Combine all ingredients except sour cream. Stir until sugar is dissolved. Gently fold in sour cream. Spoon over any hot cooked vegetables.

Especially good over broccoli.

Yield: ½ cup

Curried Breakfast Fruit Compote

1 (15 ounce) can sliced peaches	1 (15 ounce) jar spiced apples
1 (15 ounce) can sliced pears	1 tablespoon cornstarch
1 (20 ounce) can pineapple chunks	2 tablespoons brown sugar
	1 teaspoon curry powder

Years ago Betsy Steketee made this compote for a Sunday summer brunch. Great on pancakes or waffles. Also goes great with a ham dinner.

Cut fruit into bite-size pieces and place in a medium saucepan. Stir in cornstarch, sugar and curry. Cook over medium heat until fruit is warmed through and juices thicken slightly.

Yield: 8 to 10 servings

Main Dishes

Seafood, Pork, Beef, Lamb, Poultry, Vegetarian

John Silver

Throw a Starfish

*"Where there is great love
there are always miracles."*

—WILLA CATHER

Once upon a time there was a wise man who used to go to the ocean to do his writing. He had a habit of walking on the beach for inspiration before beginning his work. One day as he was walking along, he saw a human figure down the beach moving like a dancer. He smiled to himself to think of someone dancing to the day. So, he began to walk faster to catch up to the figure. As he got closer, he saw that it was a young man and the young man wasn't dancing, but instead he was reaching down to the shore, picking up something and very gently throwing it into the ocean. As he got closer he called out, "Good morning! What are you doing?" The young man paused, looked up and replied, "Throwing starfish in the ocean!" "I guess," said the man, "I should have asked, why are you throwing starfish in the ocean?" The young man replied, "The sun is up and the tide is going out. If I don't throw them in, they will die." "But, young man, don't you realize that there are miles and miles of beach and starfish all along it. You can't possibly make a difference!" The young man listened politely, then bent down, picked up another starfish and threw it into the sea, past the breaking waves and said—"It made a difference to that one."

Herb Breading for Lighter Fleshed Fish (such as Cod or Drum)

1 sleeve saltine crackers
2 tablespoons chopped parsley
1 tablespoon chopped dill
2 fish fillets, cleaned
   oil

In a food processor, purée saltine crackers until flour-like. Add herbs and purée until well mixed. If you do not have a food processor, crush crackers in their plastic sleeve until well broken up, pour into a bowl and mash with a spoon until you can't get the pieces any smaller, then chop herbs up fine and mix with the mashed saltine crackers. Next, in a skillet, heat enough oil for frying the fillets until the oil is just smoking. Dredge the fish in the crumb mix until thoroughly coated. Place fillets in oil, skin side down for two minutes, then flip and cook other side for two minutes. Check inside for doneness. Flip again every two minutes until done.

Temperature of oil is critical - keep it hot but don't deep fry. Also you may sear the flesh, place on oiled broiler pan and into a 375 degree preheated oven until done.

Yield: 2 servings

When [Jesus] had finished speaking, he said to Simon, "Put out into deep water and let down the nets for a catch."

Luke 5: 4.

Batter for Firmer Fleshed Fish (such as Rockfish and Flounder)

2	fish fillets, skinned	1	teaspoon cayenne pepper
½	cup all-purpose flour	1	egg
½	cup corn meal	1	cup milk
1	tablespoon salt		oil

"Drum. The name derives from a sound, a dull thump-thump the fish makes by vibrating muscles around its swim bladders. Some people refer to the species as redfish because of its coppery color; others call it channel bass because of its habit of feeding in deep holes. At weights of forty and ninety pounds, drum is the cape's trophy, the blue marlin of the beach... Once a drum takes a piece of bait, it swims straight toward the beach or straight to sea. To land it, an angler must set the hook firmly and quickly take in slack line."

From Hatteras Journal *by Jan DeBlieu, 1987.*

Rinse fillets in water, pat dry and set aside. Mix flour, corn meal, salt and pepper together well. Place half this mixture onto a plate. In another bowl, whisk together the egg and milk until thoroughly combined. Heat oil in a skillet until oil starts smoking. Place fillets, one at a time on the plate and coat completely one side, then the other side of the fillet in this mix, shaking off excess. Dip each fillet into the egg and milk wash then dredge in the second half of the breading mixture, coating the entire fillet. Place fillets skin side down in skillet. Turn after two minutes and cook other side for two minutes. Check inside for doneness. Flip again every two minutes until done. Flesh is done when all inside is white and a constant color. Do not be fooled by blood lines.

This is also a classic battered fish dish for deep frying. Mix wet and dry together until batter adheres to the fish without being too sticky and ripping up the fish.

Yield: 2 servings

Fish Filet Florentine

8 ounces soft cream cheese with olives and pimento	4 flounder or sole fillets, 4 ounces each
1 (10 ounce) package frozen chopped spinach, thawed and squeezed dry	1 tablespoon milk ½ teaspoon lemon juice ⅛ teaspoon pepper paprika

Mix ¾ cup cream cheese and the spinach in a small bowl. Mound the cream cheese and spinach mixture across the middle of each fillet, distributing it evenly between the four fillets. Roll or tuck the fish around the filling and place seam side down in a greased baking dish. In a small bowl add milk, lemon juice and pepper to remaining cream cheese and stir until smooth. Spoon over fish rolls and top with paprika. Bake at 375 degrees for 20 minutes (sauce on top should be browned).

Yield: 4 servings

Quick and Easy Dolphin Marinara

2 eggs	¼ cup olive oil
1½ cups Italian Progresso bread crumbs	1½ cups mozzarella cheese
2 pounds Dolphin (or Grouper), cut into serving size pieces	1 (26 ounce) jar Paul Newman's Marinara Sauce

Preheat oven to 350 degrees. Beat eggs thoroughly in a bowl. In a second bowl place the bread crumbs. Dip each fish piece into first the eggs, then the bread crumbs to coat the fish. Lightly fry each piece in olive oil to just brown on all sides. Do not cook all the way. Layer the lightly cooked fish in a greased casserole dish. Cover all fish completely with the cheese and then the entire jar of sauce. Bake at 350 degrees until bubbly. Serve with spaghetti or linguini noodles and Italian bread.

Yield: 6 servings

"*The immersion in ocean water killed all but the marsh grasses and left the island's profile even flatter than it is today. Compared to other barrier islands on the North American Atlantic seaboard, the Outer Banks were anomalies — unusually thin and unusually low, little more than well-developed shoals colonized by a few hardy species of plants.*"

From Hatteras Journal *by Jan DeBlieu, 1987.*

Baked Marinated Fish

4	pounds mild flavored fish steaks	4	sliced tomatoes, large and fresh
12	tablespoons olive oil	1	tablespoon ground dill
12	tablespoons lemon juice	1	tablespoon ground thyme
1½	teaspoons salt	1	tablespoon ground bay
¼	teaspoon curry	1	tablespoon ground parsley
¼	teaspoon ground oregano		
1	cup diced green onions		lemon and lime slices for garnish

Marinate fish in the next six ingredients for 4 to 6 hours in the refrigerator, turning steaks over frequently. After marinating is done, preheat oven to 400 degrees. In a lightly greased baking dish, place the sliced tomatoes in a layer, then remove fish from marinade and place in single layer on top of tomatoes. Pour marinade over fish and sprinkle with dill, thyme, bay and parsley. Bake at 400 degrees for about 30 minutes until fish is done.

Yield: 4 servings

Marinated Grilled Tuna Steak

4	fresh tuna steaks, 1¼ inch thick	1	tablespoon honey or sugar
1	cup orange juice	1	tablespoon ground ginger
¼	cup soy sauce	1	tablespoon Coleman's dry mustard
¼	cup olive oil		
¼	cup white wine	1	tablespoon minced garlic
¼	cup Triple-Sec Liqueur		

Place tuna in a plastic bag. Mix all remaining ingredients in a bowl with a whisk and pour over tuna. Place bag in refrigerator for minimum or 2 hours or overnight. Turn bag once or twice. Remove from refrigerator and bring to room temperature before grilling. Grill about five minutes per side. Be careful not to overcook. Fish should be firm but interior should still be juicy.

Yield: 4 servings

Baked Fish Piquant

2	pounds fish fillets	1	cup mayonnaise
2	cups white dinner wine	1	cup dairy sour cream
2	tablespoons salt	½	cup chopped onion
	bread crumbs, dry and fine		paprika

Marinate fish in wine and salt for about 2 hours. After marinated, preheat oven to 500 degrees. Drain thoroughly on paper towels. Dip both sides of fillets in bread crumbs and arrange side by side in a shallow, greased baking dish. Mix mayonnaise, sour cream and onion then spread this mixture evenly over fish. Cover with thin layer of bread crumbs. Dust top with paprika. Bake in hot oven, 500 degrees for ten minutes or until fish flakes with a fork.

Yield: 6 servings

Any Fish Sauté

2-3	shallots, minced	4	cups orange section, halved
4	cloves garlic, minced		
2	tablespoons olive oil	2	cups fresh watercress
1	cup dry white wine	4	slices bacon, cooked and crumbled
1	tablespoon grated orange rind	⅓	cup pecan halves, toasted

Sauté shallots and garlic in hot olive oil for 2 to 3 minutes until tender. Add wine and stir occasionally until contents are reduced to about ¼ cup. Add orange rind, orange sections and watercress and stir while cooking constantly until oranges and heated and watercress is slightly wilted. Stir in bacon and pecans.

This refreshing sauce dish is delicious with any fish (or even light chicken) recipe.

Yield: 6 cups

"Wind is culture and heritage on the Outer Banks; wind shapes earth, plant, animal, human. Wind toughens us, moves mountains of sand as we watch, makes it difficult to sleepwalk through life."

From Wind *by Jan DeBlieu, 1998.*

Mary Ann's Shrimp

2	sticks butter	2	lemons, juice of
2	tablespoons parsley	2	teaspoons black pepper
1½	teaspoons basil	1½	tablespoons liquid crab boil
½	teaspoon oregano		
1½	teaspoons garlic powder	3	pounds large shrimp in shells (about 25 shrimp to the pound)
1½	teaspoons salt		

Preheat oven to 400 degrees. Melt butter in a large baking dish and mix in everything except the shrimp. Stir in shrimp and bake uncovered in oven at 400 degrees until done, about 10 minutes. Serve with pan juices, lots of paper napkins and lots of French bread to sop up juice.

Yield: 6 servings

Low Country Shrimp

2	cups shrimp, cooked and cleaned	2	cups rice, cooked as per package directions
2	tablespoons Worcestershire sauce	1	teaspoon salt
½	cup bell pepper, chopped	½	teaspoon black pepper
½	cup celery, chopped		Tabasco sauce, to taste
1	medium onion, chopped	4	slices bacon, cooked, drained of grease and crumbled
3	tablespoons butter or margarine		

Sprinkle shrimp with Worcestershire sauce and let stand 20 minutes. While standing, sauté bell pepper, celery and onion in butter until onion is clear. Add shrimp, cooked rice, salt, pepper and Tabasco to skillet with cooked vegetables, removing from heat. Toss well. Turn into a bowl and sprinkle top with bacon crumbs. May add more seasonings to taste.

Yield: 6 servings

Shrimp with Bow Ties and Beans

1	cup bow tie pasta	3-4	sprigs fresh rosemary
½	pound cannellini beans, canned or fresh	2-3	roma tomatoes, diced
4	ounces olive oil	6	ounces chicken stock
1	pound shrimp, cleaned and deveined (20-25 medium size shrimp)	4	teaspoons grated cheese (Asiago, Parmesan or Romano)
	salt and pepper to taste	4	teaspoons chopped parsley
2	cloves garlic, minced		

Cook pasta as directed by package to an "al dente" condition, then drain and set aside. Warm the canned beans in another pan and, again, do not overcook. In a large saucepan or deep skillet, heat 2 ounces of the oil. Sauté shrimp in warm oil with salt and pepper to season for about one minute. Stir in minced garlic, rosemary, and diced tomatoes and cook over medium heat for about one minute. Be careful not to burn the garlic. Drain the beans reserving ¼ cup of juice. Add beans and this reserved juice to shrimp mixture. Add the chicken stock, pasta and last 2 ounces of olive oil. Heat for about two minutes. A light sauce will form. Divide into 4 heated pasta bowls with 1 teaspoon of grated cheese sprinkled on top of each and one teaspoon of parsley on top of the cheese for each bowl. Serve immediately with bread and a garden salad.

Yield: 4 servings

"We all have our favorite winds. Outer Banks surf casters like a land breeze because, as they say, 'Wind from the east, fish bite the least. Wind from the west, fish bite the best.' A westerly breeze draws trout, mullet, and other species to the calm waters in the lee of the shore. During duck hunting season it also pushes waterfowl from the middle of Pamlico sound toward the islands, putting them in easy range of hunting blinds."

From Wind by Jan DeBlieu, 1998.

Shrimp and Grits

Grits

4	cups water	½	cup grated Parmesan cheese
1	cup grits (not instant)		white cayenne pepper (red will do)
½	teaspoon salt		ground nutmeg
4	tablespoons butter		
1	cup grated sharp cheddar cheese		

Shrimp

1	pound shrimp peeled	1	clove garlic, large and pressed
6	slices bacon, diced	4	teaspoons lemon juice
	peanut or canola oil		chopped fresh (dried is okay) parsley, to taste
2	cups sliced mushrooms		Tabasco sauce, to taste
1	cup sliced scallions (green onions)		salt and pepper, to taste

Rev. Charles Gill submitted this recipe with a note "Ahh! Southern delight, with thanks to Sis Cheshire and other Southerners."

Bring water to a boil, stir in grits and reduce heat. Stir frequently for 20 minutes or according to package directions until grits are thick and tender. Stir in salt, butter, cheese, pepper and nutmeg. While grits are cooking, wash shrimp and pat dry with paper towels and set aside. Cook diced bacon in a large skillet until crisp. Drain bacon and reserve drippings. With bacon drippings returned to the skillet, add oil until a thin, complete layer forms across bottom and heat. When oil is hot, add shrimp. When shrimp turns pink, add mushrooms, scallions, garlic, lemon juice, parsley, Tabasco, salt and pepper. Stir gently but thoroughly. Divide grits onto four warm plates or large plate bowls and spoon shrimp mixture over the grits and serve.

Yield: 4 servings

Sweet and Sour Shrimp

⅓ cup teriyaki sauce

3 tablespoons frozen pineapple juice concentrate

1½ tablespoons rice vinegar

hot sauce, to taste

½ teaspoon cornstarch

½ fresh pineapple (or a 20 ounce can unsweetened pineapple chunks, drained)

1 tablespoon canola oil, divided

1 tablespoon minced gingerroot

1 pound large shrimp, peeled and deveined

1 bunch (about ½ to 1 cup) scallions (green onions), trimmed and cut to 1 inch lengths

salt, to taste

In a small bowl, whisk together the teriyaki sauce, pineapple juice concentrate, vinegar, hot sauce and cornstarch. Set aside. If using fresh pineapple, peel the half pineapple and cut into 4 lengthwise wedges, then cut again crosswise into ¼ inch thick slices. Set aside. In a wok, or large skillet, heat 1 teaspoon of the oil over high heat until very hot. Add gingerroot and stir-fry until fragrant (about 30 seconds). Add shrimp and stir-fry until shrimp turns pink (2 to 3 minutes). Transfer shrimp to a warm bowl. In same wok, heat remaining oil until very hot. Add pineapple and scallions and cook stirring occasionally until pineapple is brown in spots (about 4 minutes if using fresh pineapple). Add reserved sauce mixture and shrimp and heat through (about 1 minute). Adjust taste with salt. Serve immediately.

Yield: 4 servings

Shrimp Fried Rice

canola or peanut oil as needed

2 cups rice, cooked and chilled

1 egg

1 cup onions, chopped

½ cup green or red pepper, chopped

4-5 dried shiitake mushrooms, reconstituted and sliced (or fresh mushrooms sliced)

2-3 ounces ham, chopped (country ham is best)

12 ounces shrimp, peeled, deveined and chopped

salt and soy sauce to taste

1 cup frozen peas, defrosted

sesame oil

1 bunch scallions (green onions), sliced thinly

Put one tablespoon of oil in a large skillet or wok. Heat on low to medium and add cooked rice (as directed by rice package). Stir until each grain of rice is coated lightly with oil by adding small amounts of oil as needed. In a bowl, beat the egg and then fry in a small pan until firm. Set egg aside. To wok or skillet, add onion and pepper and stir until cooked. Add mushrooms, ham and shrimp and stir until shrimp turns pink. Add salt and or soy to taste and to color the rice. Stir in peas and warm mixture. Roll the fried egg up tightly and slice to form ¼ inch strips. Put rice and shrimp mixture in a serving bowl, sprinkle with sesame oil and then scallions. Decorate with egg slices and serve.

Cooked pork or chicken can be substituted for the shrimp.

Yield: 8 servings

Shrimp Sea Island

5 pounds shrimp, peeled and cooked then deveined of back sand membrane	1 large bottle capers with juice
	salt
	sugar
10 small to medium mild white onions sliced in thin rings	Tabasco sauce
	Worcestershire sauce
1 pint pure olive oil	lettuce leaves, parsley and lemon slices to garnish
¾ pint good cider vinegar	

Wash and drain shrimp. Alternating, starting with shrimp, layer shrimp and sliced onions in a deep, flat pan or bowl until all ingredients are used. In a separate bowl, mix oil, vinegar and capers. Season with remaining ingredients to taste, mixing thoroughly. Pour this dressing mix over shrimp and onions. Cover pan and place in refrigerator 12 hours or overnight, stirring occasionally. To serve, lift out of dressing with slotted spoon and place on large platter decorated with crisp lettuce leaves or parsley, or put shrimp and onions in a large, clear glass bowl and garnish sides and top with lemon slices.

Can use cooked tuna, cut into bite-size pieces in place of shrimp.

Yield: 8 to 10 servings

Originally this recipe was Gladys McKinnon's and published in "Coastal Cookery" but has been modified over time and with much use by Jackie Jenkins. It is a local favorite, a popular buffet dish, makes a nice salad and can be used as an appetizer as well. Jackie finds it a bit rich for a meal main dish.

Saint Martin Shrimp

4 tablespoons fresh garlic, minced

1 small to medium red onion, julienne sliced

¼ cup olive oil

1 pound shrimp, peeled and deveined

2 cups tomatoes, coarsely chopped

4 tablespoons bacon, chopped and cooked (optional)

¼ cup fresh parsley, chopped

salt and pepper, to taste

½ cup dry white wine

1 pound cooked fettuccini noodles

¼ cup butter

½ cup freshly grated Parmesan cheese

This recipe is from one of the most popular seafood pubs in the area and is published courtesy of Saint Andrew's parishioner Bob Sanders, owner/ manager, and Richard Welch, owner/chef, Tortugas' Lie Restaurant.

Sauté garlic and red onion in the olive oil over medium to high heat until soft. Add shrimp, stir and cook for one minute. Add tomato, bacon (if used), parsley, salt and pepper. Cook one more minute while continuing to stir. Add the white wine to deglaze the pan, stirring to loosen any browned bits of food. Reduce pan liquids to half volume by cooking down over medium heat while gently stirring. Stir in cooked pasta and butter and continue to cook over medium heat until pasta is hot. Served topped with grated Parmesan cheese.

Yield: 4 servings

Scallop Casserole

This recipe is from a dear friend of Joyce Pickrel's, B. Jenkins.

¼ pound butter, melted

1 (8 ounce) package Pepperidge Farm stuffing crumbs

½ teaspoon celery salt

3 cups scallops, bite-size

1 pint whipping cream

Mix melted butter, stuffing crumbs, celery salt and scallops. Whip the cream and fold it into the mixture. Place in greased baking dish and bake at 375 degrees for 35 to 40 minutes.

Yield: 6 servings

New Orleans-Style Bar-B-Que Shrimp

1	pound shrimp, shells on	½	cup lemon juice
½	cup olive oil	¼	cup Lea and Perrin sauce
2	tablespoons cracked pepper	¼	cup Tabasco sauce
1	tablespoon salt	½	cup butter

Rinse shrimp in clear water then pat dry with paper towels. Place shrimp in a single layer on a baking sheet which has raised edges. Drizzle with olive oil. Pepper and salt shrimp. Add lemon juice, Lea and Perrin and Tabasco sauces by drizzling over shrimp. Cut up butter and scatter on top of shrimp. Broil 15 to 20 minutes.

Yield: 4 servings

Crab Quiche

2	pie shells, deep dish	3	eggs
1	pound lump crabmeat, coarsely shredded	8	ounces sour cream
		1½	cup sharp cheddar cheese
1	can large fried onion rings	⅛	teaspoon Tabasco sauce

Preheat oven to 350 degrees. Into pie shells, layer crabmeat and onion rings. In blender, mix eggs, sour cream, cheese and Tabasco. Divide and pour blended mixture evenly into the two pie shells. Bake at 350 degrees for about 35 minutes.

Yield: 8 to 12 servings

"Chicamacomico Banks — which perhaps was too long to suit postal officials — became Rodanthe after a small violet or pink flower with a yellow center. Also known as Helipterum or Swan Lake everlasting, its designation as the town namesake was, to many Chicamacomico residents, a source of continued irritation... Its range as a wildflower is limited to western Australia. It has never bloomed on the Outer Banks."

From Hatteras Journal *by Jan DeBlieu, 1987.*

Maryland Eastern Shore Crab Cakes

¼ cup cracker meal	½ teaspoon Old Bay seasoning
¼ cup mayonnaise	
1 egg, lightly beaten	1 pound lump crabmeat, coarsely shredded
1 tablespoon onion, minced	
¼ teaspoon Worcestershire sauce	4 tablespoons butter or margarine
¼ teaspoon dry mustard	½ cup fresh bread crumbs

Combine first seven ingredients. Pour over crabmeat and toss gently. Heat butter in large skillet. Form crab into 4 to 6 patties and roll in bread crumbs. Fry at medium to high heat until golden brown and serve with your favorite sauce.

Yield: 4 to 6 servings

Stuffed Clams

2 dozen large fresh quahaug clams, scrubbed and steamed	⅛ teaspoon black pepper, freshly ground
	chili powder "pinch"
1 egg	4 unsalted soda crackers
½ cup cream (half-and-half)	canola oil
1 tablespoon onion, minced	butter, melted
¼ teaspoon salt	paprika or chopped pimiento

Preheat oven to 400 degrees. Drain steamed clams, reserving the juice. Open and remove clams, putting shells aside to dry. Put cooked clams, clam juice, egg and cream into blender on medium speed or about 5 seconds. With blender running, quickly add onion, salt, pepper, chili powder and crackers. Blend for a few seconds until well mixed. Oil clam shells with the canola oil. Heap some of the clam mixture into each shell, drizzle butter generously over top and garnish with paprika or pimiento. Bake quickly in a hot oven (400 degrees) for about 15 minutes.

Yield: 2 (1-dozen) servings, or 24 stuffed half shells

Maryland Crab Imperial

Filling

1 pound lump or backfin crabmeat, coarsely shredded

6 soda crackers, crushed into fine crumbs

1-2 tablespoons green pepper, finely chopped

1 egg

2 tablespoons mayonnaise

1 teaspoon white Worcestershire sauce

2 drops Tabasco sauce

¼ cup fresh parsley, finely chopped

salt and pepper, to taste

4 individual serving baking shells or ramekins

Glaze

½ cup mayonnaise

1 teaspoon prepared mustard

¼ teaspoon lemon juice

Preheat oven to 425 degrees. Place crabmeat, soda cracker crumbs, and green pepper in mixing bowl. In a separate bowl beat the egg with the 2 tablespoons mayonnaise, Worcestershire and Tabasco sauce. Blend this into crabmeat bowl. Add parsley, salt and pepper. Divide mixture into four portions and mound into baking shells or ramekins. Blend together glaze ingredients and glaze each serving's surface. Place on baking sheet or in shallow pan and bake at 425 degrees for about 20 minutes or until lightly browned. Serve immediately.

Yield: 4 servings

Lillian Lewis' Fried Oysters

½	cup all-purpose flour	1	pint shucked oysters,
⅛	teaspoon paprika		reserve liquor
1	teaspoon baking powder		cooking oil
1	egg, beaten		

Mix flour, paprika, baking powder and egg to form a batter, moistening with oyster liquor. Dip oysters into batter and fry in a skillet with about ½ inch depth hot oil, until golden brown. Serve immediately.

If not enough oyster liquor to form a proper batter, milk may be used as well. The baking powder gives the oysters a tempura-like batter.

Yield: 4 servings

Lisa Armstrong submitted this recipe with this story: Lillian's husband, John, was an old-fashioned Chesapeake Bay waterman who hand-tonged for oysters in the Rappahannock River and Bay in the 1930-1950 time frame. This was "her" way to fry them.

Scalloped Scallops

2	tablespoons butter	2	pounds scallops
6-8	saltine crackers		half-and-half or cream
4	slices (or more if needed) soft, white bread		parsley

Preheat oven to 400 degrees. Melt butter in skillet and lightly brown crumbs and the bread slices. In a buttered casserole dish, layer crumb/bread mixture, then scallops, then crumb/bread ending with crumb/bread. Pour in just enough half-and-half to fill to the top edge of dish. Bake at 400 degrees for about 20 minutes or until browned on top. Sprinkle with dried parsley or garnish with fresh parsley just before serving.

Yield: 4 servings

This recipe is that of a good friend of Vera Evans, Aletha Godwin, "who never could give me exact measures. I found that this is good no matter what you do to it!"

Danish Meat Balls or Frikadeller

½ pound ground sirloin
½ pound ground lean pork
1 medium onion, finely chopped
3 tablespoons flour
1 cup milk

1 egg, beaten
1 teaspoon salt
½ teaspoon pepper
   Worcestershire sauce, optional
3 ounces butter

Blend together the meats and onion. Add flour and mix thoroughly. Gradually add the milk, two tablespoons at a time, mixing constantly to aerate the mixture. Beat in egg, salt, pepper and Worcestershire sauce, if desired. Using two teaspoons dipped into hot water, shape mixture into oval balls. Melt butter into skillet and cook meat balls on all sides until browned all over.

Yield: 4 servings

For a traditional Danish meal, Jane Berry serves these with sugar-browned potatoes and red cabbage. She has the butcher's shop or store meat department put the sirloin and pork through the grinder twice.

Sausage and Apples

1 Kielbasa or Polish sausage, large
1 onion, large
2 Granny Smith apples, cored and peeled

½ teaspoon nutmeg
   salt and pepper to taste
¼ cup water
   skillet with cover

Slice into bite-size or slightly smaller pieces the sausage, onion and apples. Sauté in skillet (if more oil needed than in sausage, spray lightly with non-stick spray). Add seasoning and cook on medium heat for about 10 minutes. Add water, cover and simmer for another 10 minutes. Serve with rice or noodles.

Yield: 2 to 4 servings

Phyllis' Favorite Lasagna

1 pound Italian sausage, regular or turkey	3 cups shredded mozzarella cheese
15 ounces whole, skim or fat-free ricotta cheese	32 ounces marinara sauce
1-2 eggs	12 cooked lasagna noodles
	1 9 x 13 inch pan

Give food to the hungry, O Lord, and hunger for You to those who have food.

Unknown.

Preheat oven to 350 degrees. Remove sausage from casings and brown, crumbling as you cook. Drain fat and set aside. In a bowl, mix ricotta with 1 beaten egg, if using whole, or with 2 beaten eggs if using skim or fat-free ricotta. Add parsley and fold in 1½ cups of mozzarella cheese. In the 9 x 13 pan, pour 1 cup of marinara sauce along the bottom. Layer in four noodles. Spread half the ricotta mixture evenly over noodle. Sprinkle half the sausage over this. Pour 1 cup marinara over this and layer four more noodles. Repeat the ricotta and sausage layers. Pour 1 cup marinara sauce over these. Layer last four noodles and pour last 1 cup marinara sauce over this. Sprinkle evenly over top the last 1½ cups mozzarella cheese. Bake 20 to 30 minutes. Cheese should be melted. Allow lasagna to stand at least 30 minutes.

Really tastes better if refrigerated until the next day and then reheated. Also can be frozen after cooking for a later date.

Yield: 6 to 8 servings

Sausage Pasta Fagioli with Spinach

1 pound sweet Italian sausage, casings removed
1 tablespoon olive oil
2 medium onions, chopped
2 garlic cloves, minced
1 (28 ounce) can plum tomatoes in juice

2 (13-14 ounce) cans of chicken broth
3 (15 ounce) cans cannellini beans, rinsed and drained
6 ounces tube pasta
1 (10 ounce) bag fresh spinach, stems removed and torn into 1 inch strips

Heat heavy 5 quart sauce pan over medium heat. Add sausage and cook until browned. Break meat up with spoon. With slotted spoon remove meat from pan and set aside. Using pan drippings and olive oil, cook onions until tender, about 10 minutes. Add garlic and cook for 1 minute. Add tomatoes with juice, using spoon to break up large chunks. Add chicken broth and beans. Heat to boiling and then simmer for 15 minutes. Add sausage and heat through. Meanwhile, in a 3 quart saucepan, cook pasta according to label and drain pasta. Just before serving, stir in spinach and cooked pasta into 5 quart pan and heat until spinach is tender.

Serve with Parmesan cheese, crusty Italian bread and a hearty Italian wine.

Yield: 6 to 8 servings

He turned the desert into pools of water and the parched ground into flowing springs; there he brought the hungry to live and they founded a city they could settle. They sowed fields and planted vineyards that yielded a fruitful harvest; he blessed them and their numbers greatly increased, and he did not let their herds diminish.

Psalm 107: 35-38.

Blackstrap Molasses Pork Tenderloin

2	trimmed pork tenderloins (about 2 pounds)	2	tablespoons butter, softened
¼	cup molasses	1	teaspoon black pepper
2	tablespoons brown sugar	1	tablespoon salt
		1	teaspoon Tabasco
		2	tablespoons oil or butter

Cut tenderloins into 2 ounce medallions. Pound medallions lightly just so meat spreads slightly. Place in a single layer on a tray. In a bowl, combine all other ingredients, except the 2 tablespoons of oil or butter, and whisk into a combined consistency. Coat pork medallions liberally with this marinade. Let set refrigerated for two to four hours. In a large skillet, heat the oil or butter. Sear medallions in this skillet for about 1 minute on each side, caramelizing the sugars.

Yield: 4 servings

Louise's Beef Stew

3	tablespoons flour	1	(16 ounce) can tomatoes
1	teaspoon salt	3	medium onions, sliced
½	teaspoon celery salt	⅓	cup red wine vinegar
¼	teaspoon garlic salt	½	cup molasses
¼	teaspoon pepper	½	cup water
½	teaspoon ginger	6	carrots, cut on diagonal into chunks
3	pounds beef chuck, cut in 2 inch cubes	½	cup raisins
2	tablespoons cooking oil		

Combine first 6 ingredients and sprinkle over beef cubes. Brown beef in hot oil. Remove to a Dutch oven and add tomatoes, onions, vinegar, molasses and water. Bring to a boil, cover and simmer for about 2 hours. Add carrots and raisins and simmer covered another 30 minutes or until carrots are tender. Serve with mashed potatoes or noodles.

Yield: 8 to 10 servings

Grilled Chuck Roast

1	cup Italian dressing (recommend Wishbone)	1	chuck roast, 2½ inches thick (about 3 to 4 pounds)
1	teaspoon soy sauce	2	tablespoons ketchup
1	teaspoon lemon juice	1	teaspoon A-1 or similar steak sauce
3	tablespoons sherry	1	teaspoon Worcestershire sauce

Mix Italian dressing, soy, lemon juice and sherry together. Marinate chuck roast in this for 24 hours, turning frequently. Remove roast from marinade. To the marinade, add ketchup, A-1 and Worcestershire sauce. Mix. Place roast in a roasting pan and pour a little marinade on the roast. Use remaining marinade to baste roast as it cooks. Cook meat over a hot charcoal or gas grill for 40 minutes, turning and basting roast frequently. Meat will brown on the outside and be medium-rare to rare on the inside. Cook longer if desired. Slice thinly against grain of the meat.

Yield: 6 to 8 servings

Lamb Shanks

	lamb shanks, one per person served	2	tablespoons Worcestershire sauce
	oil	½	tablespoon cider vinegar
1-2	large onions, sliced thin	¼	cup brown sugar
4	cloves garlic	2	teaspoons dry mustard
1	cup ketchup	1	cup golden raisins
1	cup water		

Preheat oven to 350 degrees. Brown lamb shanks in oil and drain. In a deep dish casserole, place browned lamb shanks and cover with sliced onions. In a bowl, mix the remaining ingredients together well. Pour over lamb and onions. Bake at 350 degrees for 2 to 2½ hours.

Yield: servings equal number of lamb shanks cooked

The Alpha Stew

1	good size chuck roast (3 to 3½ pounds)
6	medium potatoes, coarsely chopped
4	medium onions, coarsely chopped
6	large carrots, coarsely chopped
1	package dry French onion soup mix
1	can warm beer (8-12 ounces)
	salt and pepper, to taste

Preheat oven to 400 degrees. Place roast in a casserole dish. Salt and pepper to taste, add chopped vegetables on top of roast. Sprinkle entire dish with dry soup mix and pour beer over contents. Cover with casserole dish lid or cover tightly with aluminum foil. Cook at 400 degrees for 10 minutes, reduce heat to 300 degrees and cook another 3 hours.

For tougher roasts, excellent in a crock pot on low setting after browning meat first. Longer cooked on low, the more tender it will be. Can be prepared a head of time and warmed up before serving in oven or in microwave.

Yield: 6 servings

Hamburger Pie

2   (8 ounce) cans tomato
      sauce
½   cup bread crumbs
¼   cup onions, chopped
1½ teaspoons salt
⅛   teaspoon pepper
1   pound ground beef
¼   cup chopped green pepper

1⅓ cup quick cook (Minute)
      rice, uncooked
1   cup salted water
      (½ teaspoon salt in
      1 cup water)
1   cup cheddar cheese,
      grated or shredded

Preheat oven to 350 degrees. Combine ½ cup of the tomato sauce with the next six ingredients. Mix well. Pat meat mixture into the bottom and sides of an 8 inch greased, glass baking dish and set aside. Combine rice, remaining tomato sauce, the salted water and ¼ of the cup of cheese. Spoon this mixture into the hamburger shell. Cover with aluminum foil and bake at 350 degrees for 25 minutes. Uncover, sprinkle top with remaining cheese and return to oven, uncovered. Bake another 10 to 15 minutes.

Yield: 4 servings

Bring the fattened calf and kill it. Let us have a feast and celebrate.

Luke 15: 23.

Cheesy Chicken

3	sauce pans	1	pound butter
6	eggs	4	cups bread crumbs
2	(13 ounce) cans evaporated milk	½	pound shredded mozzarella cheese
2	cups water	12	boneless, skinless chicken breasts, washed and drained
1	tablespoon cinnamon		
½	cup sugar		hollandaise sauce, optional
	salt and pepper to taste		

This is a favorite from the Chef at Cobb's Restaurant in Williamston, North Carolina. Carol Brassington highly recommends using the hollandaise sauce to really set off the flavors of this gourmet dish.

Preheat oven to 350 degrees. In the first sauce pan mix eggs, milk, water, cinnamon, sugar, salt and pepper. In the second sauce pan, melt the butter. In the third saucepan mix bread crumbs and cheese. Place chicken breasts in the first pan for a few minutes. Then, one at a time, dip each breast in the butter and next roll in bread crumb and cheese pan to coat evenly. Shape each coated breast into a ball and place on greased baking dish or pan. Bake for about 40 minutes at 350 degrees. Bake covered for moist chicken and uncovered for crunchy. Serve with hollandaise sauce, if desired

Try the Sour Cream Sauce for Vegetables found elsewhere in this cookbook on the chicken instead of the hollandaise for a tasty change.

Yield: 12 servings

Chicken Pineapple Cheese Supreme

1 (9 or 10 ounce) package frozen broccoli spears	⅛ teaspoon pepper
4 boneless, skinless chicken breasts, washed and drained	2 tablespoons margarine or butter
3 tablespoons all-purpose flour	1 (8 ounce) can pineapple slices, drained
½ teaspoon salt	4 (1 ounce) slices of Monterey Jack, Swiss, or provolone cheese

Cook broccoli as directed on package, then drain. Place each chicken breast between two pieces of plastic wrap or wax paper and working from the center, gently pound the chicken with flat side of meat mallet or rolling pin until about ¼ inch thick. In a shallow pan, mix flour, salt and pepper. Coat each flattened breast with this mixture. Melt margarine or butter in a skillet and cook breasts on medium heat for 5 to 6 minutes on each side or until chicken is fork-tender and juices run clear. Place a pineapple slice on top of each chicken breast and top each pineapple slice with broccoli, evenly distributing the broccoli among the four breasts. Place one slice of cheese on each, cover skillet and cook an additional 1 minute on medium heat or until cheese is melted.

Yield: 4 servings

Connie's Chicken Orange

1 whole fryer cut up
½ cup shortening
½ teaspoon paprika
2 tablespoons brown sugar
2 tablespoons chopped parsley

2 tablespoons soy sauce
½ teaspoon ground nutmeg
⅓ cup water
½ cup frozen orange juice concentrate
1 large onion, sliced

Brown chicken in shortening. Place chicken in casserole. Combine remaining ingredients, except onion, in a saucepan and warm on low until orange juice is melted. Cover chicken in casserole with sliced onion and pour sauce over all. Bake in slow (275 to 325 degree) oven until tender, about an hour.

If you want to cut calories, skin the chicken and skip the browning.

Yield: 4 servings

Italian Chicken

6 boneless, skinless chicken breasts, washed and drained
½ pound provolone cheese, in form of six slices

½ pound Italian ham, in form of six slices
6 ounces mozzarella cheese, shredded
1 (26 ounce) jar spaghetti sauce

Preheat oven to 350 degrees. Pound chicken breasts until thin and flat. Place one slice of provolone and one slice of Italian ham on each breast and roll up. Place the six rolled breasts in a baking dish. Pour spaghetti sauce over the top. Place mozzarella cheese over the top of this and cover dish with aluminum foil. Bake at 350 degrees for about 1 hour or until chicken is cooked through. Remove foil for last ten minutes to brown cheese.

Yield: 6 servings

Spinach Chicken Roll

6   boneless, skinless
chicken breasts
1   (10 ounce) package
frozen chopped
spinach, thawed
16 ounces ricotta cheese
1   egg

Italian bread crumbs,
canned
toothpicks
1   stick butter
2   (10¾ ounce) cans cream
of chicken soup,
undiluted

Preheat oven to 375 degrees. Pound chicken breasts flat.
Place spinach, ricotta cheese and egg in bowl and mix well.
Spoon mixture onto chicken breasts and spread, dividing
mixture evenly between the breasts. Roll breasts and fasten
to hold them together with toothpicks. Roll the breast rolls
in the bread crumbs. Fry in pan with butter until browned
on all sides. Place browned chicken rolls in a baking dish
and cover with cream of chicken soup. Bake at 375 degrees
for 45 minutes to one hour.

Yield: 6 servings

*Margaret
Hunt says this is
"My favorite way
to serve this dish is
with a pound of
egg noodles boiled
while the chicken
is baking. I place
the chicken rolls
on top of the
noodles and
garnish with
parsley."*

Chicken Mushroom Artichoke Casserole

Mary Bobbit likes this recipe because it can be made the day before, following the directions up to adding the cheese on top, and refrigerated. The next day all you have to do is preheat the oven, add the cheese and bake. Great for dinner parties.

4 cups cut up chicken, bite-size

2 (10½ ounce) cans chicken stock (or favorite chicken herbs in about 2 cups water)

1 (14 ounce) package broad egg noodles

1 cup fresh mushrooms, sliced

2 tablespoons butter (or less)

2 (10¾ ounce) cans cream of mushroom or chicken soup

1 cup sour cream

¾ cup white wine

2 702 cans artichoke hearts, drained and cut into quarters

1 large can pitted ripe olives (about 15 ounces), each olive sliced in half

½ cup green pepper, chopped

½ cup pimento, chopped

1 large onion, chopped

1 cup grated Parmesan cheese

Preheat oven to 350 degrees. Simmer chicken in chicken stock or in water flavored with your favorite chicken flavoring herbs until tender. Drain, reserving the stock or broth. Cook noodles in the stock or broth. Drain. Sauté mushrooms in butter and set aside. Combine noodles, soup, sour cream and wine. Add cooked chicken, sautéed mushrooms and all remaining ingredients, except cheese. Blend well and place in baking dish. Add cheese to top and bake at 350 degrees for 45 minutes.

May also sauté the green pepper and onion with the mushrooms, if desired.

Yield: 12 servings

Country Captain

4	pounds chicken breasts (8 breasts)	1½	teaspoon salt
	seasoned flour (salt, pepper to taste and your favorite herbs)	½	teaspoon white pepper
		½	teaspoon thyme
		2	(18 ounce) cans tomatoes
½	cup shortening	1	tablespoon chopped parsley
2	onions, finely chopped		
2	green peppers, chopped	6	cups hot cooked rice
1	clove garlic, minced	¼	cup currents or raisins
3-4	teaspoons curry powder	¼	cup toasted almonds parsley sprigs

Louise Dollard says simply that "beautiful and impressive, this dish is well worth the effort."

Preheat oven to 350 degrees. Remove skin from chicken. Roll breasts in seasoned flour and fry in shortening until well browned in a large skillet. Remove chicken and keep warm (this is said to be the secret of this dish's success). In the remaining shortening, cook the onions, green peppers and garlic until tender. Stir in curry powder, salt, pepper and thyme. Mix well. Add tomatoes and parsley. Continue to cook until sauce is heated through. Place breasts in large casserole dish and pour sauce over chicken. Cover and bake at 350 degrees for 45 minutes or until chicken is tender. Arrange chicken in center of a platter, mounding cooked rice around chicken. Add raisins or currents into sauce (if desired) and pour over rice. Sprinkle almonds over chicken. Garnish with parsley sprigs and serve.

Yield: 8 servings

Chicken and Wild Rice

2½ tablespoons butter	¾ cup heavy cream
2½ tablespoons flour	salt and pepper to taste
1¾ cups rich chicken broth	
2 cups sliced mushrooms	¾ cup wild rice, cooked
1 tablespoon chopped shallots	1½ cup cooked, diced chicken

Preheat oven to 400 degrees. Melt 2 tablespoons butter in a saucepan and add flour, stirring with a whisk until well blended. Add broth, stirring rapidly. Simmer 15 minutes. Meanwhile, melt ½ tablespoon butter in another saucepan and add mushrooms, cook, and add shallots, cooking until most liquid evaporates. Add the cooked mushrooms and shallots to first sauce pan. Add cream, salt and pepper and continue cooking for 15 minutes. In casserole, blend together sauce, rice and chicken. Cover loosely and bake at 400 degrees for 45 minutes.

Yield: 3 to 4 servings

The Atlantic seaboard's age of piracy only lasted five years (1713-1718), and seriously affected the Outer Banks for less than twelve months of that time. In the spring of 1718, Blackbeard (also known as Edward Teach, Captain Drummond, or Thatch), moved into the area with four ships and about 400 men. He captured and plundered at least 25 ships by that fall. Blackbeard's death on November 22, 1718, at Ocracoke Inlet in battle with two British sloops, ended large scale piracy in the Outer Banks and, in fact, on the whole Atlantic coast.

Various Sources.

Easy One Dish Chicken Meal

	non-stick cooking spray	1	(10¾ ounce) can cream of chicken soup
1	container crescent rolls, 8 rolls per container	1	soup can of milk
1½	pounds cooked, chopped chicken or turkey	1	box any style prepared stuffing mix
	salt, pepper and garlic to taste	8-10	slices provolone cheese

Preheat oven to 400 degrees. Spray a 9 x 13 inch pan with non-stick cooking spray. Unroll crescent rolls and place flat in bottom of prepared pan. Place chicken on top of rolls and season with salt, pepper and garlic. In a bowl, combine soup and milk. Pour half the soup mixture over chicken. Put stuffing mix on top then the second half of soup mixture. Top with cheese slices. Bake at 400 degrees for 20 minutes, then put under broiler until cheese melts, bubbles and (watch this carefully) starts to brown slightly.

Simmer one thinly sliced carrot, two stalks diced celery and one small chopped onion in one cup of water until tender (about 15 minutes). Drain well and add these vegetables to the stuffing mix before using in the above recipe. May also add sliced mushrooms to the stuffing mix.

Yield: 4 servings

Now a wind went out from the Lord and drove quail in from the sea. It brought them down all around the camp for about 2 cubits (about three feet) above the ground, as far as a day's walk in any direction. All that day and night and all the next day the people went out and gathered quail. No one gathered less than ten homers (about 60 bushels).

Numbers 11: 31-32

Easy Chicken Cordon Bleu Casserole

¾ pound chicken breasts, boneless, skinless and slivered

4 ounces boiled ham, slivered

2 tablespoons butter or margarine

1 (10¾ ounce) can cream of chicken soup

1 cup water

1 tablespoon Dijon-style mustard, optional

1 (10 ounce) package frozen asparagus cuts, thawed

1½ cups quick (Minute) rice, dry (uncooked)

2 slices Swiss cheese cut into wedges or small squares

Using a large skillet, sauté chicken and ham in butter until chicken is lightly browned, about 5 minutes. Add soup, water, and mustard, if used. Bring to a full boil. Stir in rice. Lay cheese over top, cover and remove from heat. Let stand 5 minutes and then serve.

For microwave, omit butter and increase water to 1¾ cup instead of 1 cup. Combine chicken and ham in a microwave safe dish, cover and cook on high for 4 minutes. Stir in remaining ingredients, except cheese and cover. Cook on high another 5 minutes. Stir and cover again. Cook on high an added 2 to 5 minutes. Top with cheese, cover and let stand 5 minutes and then serve.

Yield: 4 servings

Gloria's Zucchini Pie

4	cups zucchini with peel, diced	2	tablespoons parsley
½	cup onion, diced	¼	teaspoon pepper
1	cup Bisquick mix	4	eggs, beaten
½	Parmesan cheese, grated	½	cup vegetable oil

Preheat oven to 350 degrees. Combine all ingredients except oil. Fold in oil with wooden spoon and then place mixture in an ungreased 13 x 9 inch pan or glass baking dish. Bake uncovered at 350 degrees for 20 to 25 minutes or until lightly brown on edges. Remove from oven and let stand five minutes before cutting into squares.

Yield: 6 to 8 servings

Ruth Lanyon tells us that "This is what I serve 'the girls' when we get together for luncheon. Someone always asks for the recipe. I serve it with green salad and rolls. It is also good reheated at 50 percent power in a microwave."

Squash Casserole

½	pound bacon or ¼ cup butter	2	cups mayonnaise
3	pounds yellow and or zucchini squash, halved and sliced	3	eggs
		1	slice bread, torn into small pieces
2	large onions, halved and sliced	1	cup Parmesan cheese, grated

Preheat oven to 350 degrees. If bacon is used, fry bacon and remove from pan, blot on paper towels to absorb grease, crumble and set aside. In the skillet with bacon grease or in a skillet with the butter (if bacon is not used), sauté the squash and onions until done. In a separate bowl combine the remaining ingredients and whip with wire whisk. Add cooked squash, onions, and crumbled bacon, if used, to this mixture. Pour mixture into a 9 x 12 inch pan and bake at 350 degrees for 30 to 45 minutes.

Yield: 6 to 8 servings

Aunt Alma's Sour Cream Rice

1	cup rice	1	pint sour cream
8	ounces New York sharp (cheddar) cheese, shredded	½-1	teaspoon crushed red pepper
4	teaspoons sugar		salt, to taste

Preheat oven to 300 degrees. Cook rice as directed by package. Add other ingredients. Place in lightly buttered baking dish and bake at 300 degrees for 25 to 30 minutes or until cheese is thoroughly melted.

Can be combined a day ahead, refrigerated and cooked the next day.

Yield: 4 servings

Better a meal of vegetables where there is love than a fattened calf with hatred.

Proverbs 15: 17.

Layered Ricotta Cheese Torte

1	cup low-fat ricotta cheese	½	cup grated Parmesan cheese
1	cup sour cream	½	teaspoon garlic salt
2	tablespoons fresh basil, coarsely chopped, or 1 tablespoon dried sweet basil	½	teaspoon seasoned pepper
		3	roma tomatoes, chopped
		3	fat-free tortillas, soft taco size

Preheat oven to 425 degrees. Mix together all ingredients except the tortillas. Spray a baking sheet with nonstick cooking spray. Place one tortilla on the baking sheet, spread one third the Ricotta mixture on the tortilla, put the second tortilla on top, another layer of ricotta mixture and final tortilla with last of ricotta mixture on top. Spray aluminum foil on one side with nonstick cooking spray and place sprayed side down on torte, sealing loosely foil edges to edges of baking sheet. Bake at 425 degrees for 15 to 20 minutes until warmed through. Remove from oven and let stand five minutes before cutting into wedges.

Yield: 3 servings

Still other seed fell on good soil, where it produced a crop — a hundred, sixty or thirty times what was sown.

Matthew 13: 8.

Crustless Spinach or Broccoli Quiche

1	(10 ounce) package frozen broccoli or spinach	1	teaspoon seasoned salt
2	eggs, lightly beaten	¼	teaspoon pepper
2	cups cottage cheese	2	teaspoons (or more) grated Parmesan cheese
			chives or dill, to taste

Cook and drain spinach or broccoli as per package. Mix all ingredients together, blending in spinach or broccoli at the end. Pour into a 9 or 10 inch pie dish and bake at 350 degrees for 25 minutes.

Can add more toppings as options to "fill" out the recipe such as mushrooms, fried onions, etc.

Yield: 4 to 6 servings

Vera Evans' daughter, Henrietta, can "throw this together" in a flash, almost while taking her coat off. Very satisfying with a salad and rolls.

Great Grandma's Meatless Pasta Sauce

16-20	ounces canned Italian peeled tomatoes	4-5	large mushrooms, sliced
1	tablespoon olive oil	2	cloves garlic, chopped
1	small can black olives, sliced and drained	1	large onion, chopped
		1	small can marinated artichoke hearts, optional

Drain and reserve juice from canned tomatoes. Cut up the tomatoes. In a large sauce pan sauté all the remaining ingredients in the olive oil. Add the tomatoes and cook until tender. Add the reserved canned juice. Serve in large bowls over cooked ziti or rigatoni with lots of bread and a garden salad.

Yield: 8 to 10 servings of sauce

This is Connie Mebane's Great Grandma's good and healthy meal for any season.

Spinach Lasagna Roll-Ups

1 package lasagna noodles

8 ounces mozzarella cheese, shredded

15 ounces ricotta cheese

1 egg

1 (10 ounce) package chopped, frozen spinach, thawed

1 (16 ounce) can or jar favorite spaghetti sauce

Heavenly Father, for these blessings from your store, keep me thankful evermore.

Amen.

Preheat oven to 350 degrees. Cook lasagna noodles as directed on package. Mix both cheese and egg in bowl until blended. Squeeze water out of spinach and add spinach to cheese and egg mix. Put a thin layer of spaghetti sauce in the bottom of a 13 x 9 inch baking dish. Choose twelve of the best cooked noodles and lay them out flat on wax paper. Divide the filling mix into twelve parts, spreading one part evenly along the top side of each noodle from one end to the other. Gently roll the noodles up and place them in the dish, one at a time. Pour remaining sauce over top and cover with foil. Bake at 350 degrees for one hour.

Yield: 6 servings

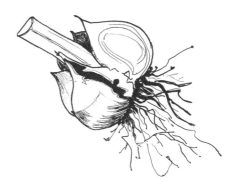

Spinach Ravioli with Fresh Spring Vegetables

½ cup pine nuts
1 teaspoon olive oil
1 large tomato, chopped
½ teaspoon salt
¼ teaspoon fresh, ground pepper
¼ cup fresh minced basil
2 (9 ounce) packages spinach ravioli
1 cup fresh peas
1 cup fresh asparagus tips

2 cups fresh broccoli florets
1 small zucchini, sliced
½ pound fresh green beans
½ pound fresh sugar snap peas
1 (6 ounce) container pesto sauce (or ¾ cup homemade)
1 cup grated Parmesan cheese

In a small sauté pan, toast pine nuts in the olive oil over medium to low heat until lightly browned. Place on paper towel to cool. Combine chopped tomato with salt, pepper, and half the basil (⅛ cup) and set aside. Cook ravioli according to package directions. Drain ravioli and place in large, warm mixing bowl. Steam all vegetables until crisp tender. Heat the pesto sauce in a saucepan. Place vegetables in the bowl with the ravioli, toss with pesto and half the cheese, half the remaining basil and half the pine nuts. Place on a warm serving platter or clean warm pasta bowl and top with the tomato mixture set aside earlier. Sprinkle with remaining cheese, basil and pine nuts.

All pasta dishes stay much hotter when tossed in a bowl heated by running under hot water and then quickly drying it.

Yield: 6 to 8 servings

Bell Pepper Confetti Macaroni and Cheese

8 ounces macaroni	3 cups skim milk
1 tablespoon olive oil	1 cup feta cheese, crumbled
1 onion, chopped	1 tablespoon dried dill
3 cloves garlic, minced	1 tablespoon Dijon-style mustard
2 red bell peppers, chopped	½ teaspoon cayenne pepper
2 yellow bell peppers, chopped	¼ teaspoon nutmeg
1 green bell pepper, chopped	salt and ground black pepper, to taste
¼ cup flour	½ cup toasted bread crumbs

Preheat oven to 400 degrees. Cook macaroni in boiling water until al dente. Drain. Sauté in olive oil the onion, garlic and bell peppers for five minutes. Stir in flour and cook one minute longer. Stir in milk and bring to a boil while stirring constantly. Reduce heat and simmer until thickened. Stir in cheese and seasonings. Stir in macaroni. Spoon entire mixture into an 8 x 12 inch baking dish that has been lightly sprayed with cooking oil. Sprinkle top with bread crumbs. Bake at 400 degrees for 30 to 40 minutes.

Yield: 6 to 8 servings

ive me good digestion, Lord, and also something to digest; Give me a healthy body, Lord, and sense to keep it at its best. Give me a healthy mind, good Lord, to keep the good and pure in sight; Which, seeing sin, is not appalled, but finds a way to set it right.

Thomas H. B. Webb.

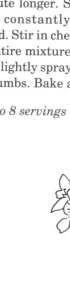

Elizabeth's Angel Hair Pasta

Dressing

¾ cup olive oil

2 tablespoons red vinegar

1¼ teaspoon garlic salt

½ teaspoon salt

⅛ teaspoon pepper

Main Dish

9 ounces angel hair pasta

4 tablespoons olive oil

½ teaspoon oregano

½ teaspoon basil

1 teaspoon salt

½ teaspoon pepper

4-5 fresh carrots, sliced into 1 inch sections then halved again lengthwise

½ pound fresh asparagus, sliced into 1 inch sections

1½ cups fresh broccoli florets

4 green onions, coarsely chopped

½ cup black olives, sliced and pitted

1 cup ham, chopped

½ cup shrimp, cooked and peeled

¼ cup feta cheese

Parmesan cheese, grated

Combine first five ingredients to make a dressing and set aside (refrigerate until needed). Cook pasta, drain, rinse and drain again. Transfer to large bowl. Add oil, oregano, basil, salt and pepper. Toss gently and set aside. Steam carrots, asparagus and broccoli for 3 to 5 minutes. Rinse vegetables under cold water and drain. Put vegetables, onions, olives, ham and shrimp on top of pasta. Add cheese. When ready to serve, coat top with as much dressing as desired. Serve with Parmesan cheese to garnish.

Yield: 6 to 8 servings

Barley Nut Delight

Dressing

1	cup green pumpkin seeds	½	teaspoon oregano
2	teaspoons lemon juice	2	teaspoons brown rice vinegar
½	teaspoon of basil	¾-1	cup water
½	teaspoon dill	1	teaspoon miso (bean paste)

Main Dish

1	cup barley, uncooked	½	cup fresh parsley, minced
⅓	cup wheat berries		
2⅔	cups spring water	½	cup roasted sunflower seeds, chopped
2	stalks celery, chopped		
1	medium onion, finely chopped	⅓	cup olive oil
		½	teaspoon sea salt
1	carrot, finely chopped		

Vanessa Foreman tells us "With its all-natural ingredients, this recipe is for good health and excellent for a healing body."

To prepare the dressing, roast seeds in a dry cast iron skillet stirring well until golden brown. Grind in a nut and seed grinder, suribachi or coffee mill. Combine lemon juice with basil, dill and oregano. Combine ground seed, lemon mix and all remaining ingredients and refrigerate. For the main dish, rinse barley and wheat berries several times and combine both with the spring water in a 1½ to 2 quart saucepan. Bring to a boil. Cover and simmer until all water is absorbed and grains are tender (approximately 50-60 minutes). Allow to cool. Mix together oil and salt. Combine all ingredients and mix thoroughly. Refrigerate for several hours before serving as is or on a bed of salad greens or stuffed in a pita with sprouts. The dressing is drizzled over this main dish salad-style meal.

Yield: 3 to 4 servings

Green Tomato Pie

1	pie crust, top and bottom, for 9 inch pie (homemade or frozen)		salt and pepper, to taste
		1	cup cheddar cheese, grated
3	medium green tomatoes	1	cup mozzarella cheese, grated
1	large onion		
1	large green bell pepper	¼	cup Parmesan cheese, grated
2	tablespoons oregano		

Preheat oven to 350 degrees. With the pie crust bottom in a pie pan ready to receive filling, slice and layer the tomatoes, onions and peppers in the pie. Sprinkle the oregano over the vegetables and lightly salt and pepper. Add all the cheese. Cover the pie with the pie crust top and cut four slits in the top crust. Bake at 350 degrees for 45 minutes.

Yield: 4 servings

We come to join in the banquet of love. Let it open our hearts and break down the fears that keep us from loving each other.

Dominican Nuns' Grace.

Red Tomato Pie

8-10	roma tomatoes or enough firm red tomatoes to fill a pie pan slightly mounded	3-4	scallions including some of the green part, chopped
		1	cup mayonnaise
1	pie shell, baked	1	cup sharp cheddar cheese, grated
1	(¾ ounce) package fresh basil, chopped		
		4-6	slices bacon, cooked and crumbled, optional

Preheat oven to 350 degrees. Slice tomatoes into slices no thinner than ¼ inch. Drain on paper towels and blot tops of slices as well. Place half of the tomato slices into the pie shell. Layer with half the basil and chopped scallions. Repeat tomato, basil and scallion layers. Mix mayonnaise and cheese in a bowl and spread mixture evenly over top of second vegetable layer. Bake at 350 degrees for 20 to 30 minutes. Garnish, if desired, with crumbled bacon.

It is very easy to burn the crust. Don't bake pie shell too long.

Yield: 4 servings

Easy Vegetarian Chili over Rice

1	tablespoon vegetable oil	1	teaspoon oregano
2	onions, chopped	½	teaspoon salt
2	carrots, diced	1	(19 ounce) can black beans, undrained
2	stalks celery, diced		
2	jalapeño peppers, chopped, optional	1	(19 ounce) can kidney beans, undrained
1	(28 ounce) can chopped tomatoes, drained	2	small zucchini, diced
		½-1	cup rice
4	cloves garlic, minced		grated cheddar cheese, optional garnish topping
1	green bell pepper, diced		
¼	cup parsley, chopped		
4	teaspoons chili powder		sour cream, optional garnish topping
1	teaspoon cumin		

In a large saucepan, heat oil over medium heat. Add onions, carrots, celery and jalapeños (if used). Stir often for six minutes. Add tomatoes, garlic, green pepper, parsley, chili powder, cumin, oregano, and salt. Bring to a simmer. Cook covered for 20 minutes, stirring often. Add beans and their juices and cook covered another 15 minutes. Add zucchini and cook uncovered for 5 minutes, stirring occasionally. Meanwhile, cook rice as per package directions (to make 5 to 6 servings). Mound cooked rice on warmed dinner plates and spoon chili on top. Sprinkle with cheese and a dollop of sour cream, if desired.

Yield: 6 servings

Mexican Vegetarian Casserole

1 (15½ ounce) can whole kernel corn, drained

1 (15 ounce) can black beans, rinsed and drained

1 (10 ounce) can whole or diced tomatoes with chilies

1 (8 ounce) container sour cream

1 (8 ounce) jar piquante sauce or salsa (pick your "heat" level)

2 cups shredded cheddar cheese

2 cups rice, cooked

¼ teaspoon pepper

1 bunch green onions, chopped

1 (2¼ ounce) can sliced ripe olives, drained

1 (8 ounce) package Monterey Jack cheese, shredded

Preheat oven to 350 degrees. Combine the first eight ingredients (corn through pepper) and spoon this mixture into a lightly greased 9 x 13 inch baking dish. Sprinkle with remaining ingredients (onions, olives and Monterey Jack cheese). Bake at 350 degrees for about 50 minutes, uncovered.

Yield: 6 servings

*For each new morning with its light,
For rest and shelter of the night,
For health and food, for love and friends,
For everything Thy goodness sends.*

Excerpt from Ralph Waldo Emerson.

Our Favorite Pizza

Crust

3	cups all-purpose flour	2½	teaspoons active dry yeast (generally one pack)
2	teaspoons salt		
1¼	cups warm tap water	4	teaspoons olive oil

Topping

2	cups canned tomatoes, chopped and well drained	1	teaspoon died oregano
		¼	cup diced onion
4	teaspoons grated Parmesan cheese	2	teaspoons garlic salt
		4	teaspoons olive oil

Prepare crust by combining flour and salt in a 2 quart bowl, leaving center "open." In a small bowl add water, yeast and let set for three minutes. Whisk together the yeast with only 1 teaspoon of the olive oil, then pour into center of 2 quart bowl. Stir with rubber spatula until soft and sticky. Very lightly flour work table and gently knead dough. Use spatula if sticks to table but do not add more flour (toughens the dough). Into a clean and dry 2 quart bowl, add the second teaspoon of olive oil and roll bowl to coat sides with oil. Form dough and roll it around in the bowl, evenly coating the dough with the oil. Cover bowl with dough with plastic wrap and let rise at room temperature for at least one hour. When risen, preheat oven to 450 degrees and well flour work table (sticking dough at this stage is bad). Divide dough in half and roll dough by pushing with right fist and pulling in a circular motion to stretch the dough with the left hand about an inch at a time until roughly the size of a 12 inch pizza pan. Using palms of hands, push dough evenly onto pizza pan that has been fully coated with oil prior to this with 1 teaspoon olive oil per pan. Place toppings on pizzas in order given in recipe. In preheated oven, bake at 450 degrees for about 30 minutes, checking every ten minutes, until edges of crust start to brown.

Yield: 2 (12 inch) pizzas.

Desserts

Cakes, Pies and Cobblers, Cookies and Brownies, Candies and Other Sweets

Sandy Ball

Cooking Companions

"No one who cooks cooks alone. Even at her most solitary, a cook in the kitchen is surrounded by generations of cooks past, the advice and menus of cooks present, the wisdom of cookbook writers."
                                                    —Laurie Colwin

No one ever actually cooks from all their cookbooks. Cookbooks are mostly flipped through and pasted with little yellow Post-it notes scribbled with "sounds good" on their pages. Cookbooks aren't so much about what's for dinner as they are about a world of abundant and creative choices. With cookbooks, our options are always open; we may not be able to speak French, but we can cook up a Gratin de Poulet au Fromage if we get the notion. When we are down in the dumps, cooking becomes therapy. Leafing through a cookbook drives the miseries away. When hearts are heavy, cooking brings comfort. Food reassures us that we will survive. If you don't believe it, butter up a hot, homemade biscuit, layer on the peach preserves, settle into a nice comfortable chair with a cup of piping hot coffee, and you own the world—all is well.

Five Flavor Pound Cake

Cake

2	sticks of butter or 16 tablespoons
½	cup vegetable shortening
3	cups sugar
5	eggs, well beaten
3	cups all-purpose flour
½	teaspoon baking powder

1	cup milk
1	teaspoon coconut extract
1	teaspoon rum extract
1	teaspoon butter extract
1	teaspoon lemon or pineapple extract
1	teaspoon vanilla extract

Glaze

1	cup sugar
½	cup water

1	teaspoon each coconut, rum, butter, vanilla and lemon or pineapple extract

We make a living by what we get, but we make a life by what we give.

Unknown.

Preheat oven to 350 degrees. Cream butter, shortening and sugar until light and fluffy. Add eggs which have been beaten until they reach a lemon color. In a separate bowl, combine flour and baking powder and add to creamed mixture alternately with the milk. Stir in all extract flavors. Spoon mixture into a greased 10 inch tube pan and bake at 350 degrees for about 1½ hours or until cake tests done. Add glaze if desired while cake is hot. Let cake and glaze set in pan about 10 minutes before turning out on a rack to cool further. Prepare glaze by combining all glaze ingredients in a heavy saucepan and bring mixture to a boil until sugar is melted.

Yield: 12 to 14 servings

Sour Cream Pound Cake

1	cup butter	3	cups flour
3	cups sugar	¼	teaspoon baking soda
1	cup sour cream	1	teaspoon almond, lemon
6	eggs, be prepared to		or rum extract
	separate yolks and	1	teaspoon vanilla extract
	whites, reserving whites		

Julie Layfield prefers the variation, where as Marylou Hogan's daughter-in-law used the basic recipe for her wedding cake. This pound cake always receives rave reviews for flavor and moistness.

Preheat oven to 300 degrees. Cream butter and sugar in a bowl until fluffy. Mix in sour cream. Add two egg yolks, one yolk at a time, beating well with each addition. Add flour and mix. Add two more egg yolks, one yolk at a time, beating well with each addition. Add baking soda and mix. Add last two egg yolks, one yolk at a time, beating well with each addition. Add flavorings and mix. In a separate bowl, beat all six egg whites until stiff. Fold or gently mix stiff egg whites into cake batter. Pour into a 10 inch tube cake pan and bake at 300 degrees for 1½ hours on lowest oven rack.

May substitute other flavorings to vary the taste.

Yield: 10 to 12 servings

Bourbon-Chocolate Torte

Cake

1 10 inch springform pan	1½ cups unsalted butter, softened
12 ounces semisweet chocolate squares, chopped	1½ cups sugar
	12 large eggs
1 (16 ounce) package pecan shortbread cookies	⅓ cup bourbon
	1 tablespoon powdered sugar

Bourbon Cream Sauce

2 large eggs	2 tablespoons sugar
¾ cup half-and-half	2 tablespoons bourbon

Gayle Summa likes to add a special touch and garnish this cake with fresh cut flowers.

Preheat oven to 350 degrees. Prepare springform pan by greasing it and then lining it with parchment paper and greasing the paper. In a glass dish, at 50 percent power, melt the chocolate pieces in a microwave. Place cookies in a food processor and process until finely ground. Set aside. Process butter, sugar and eggs until smooth. Add bourbon and melted chocolate. Blend. Fold into ground cookies. Pour total mixture into prepared springform pan and bake at 350 degrees for about 1 hour. Cool on a wire rack in the pan for about 30 minutes. Cover and chill in pan for about 8 hours. Remove from pan and sprinkle with powdered sugar. Before serving, prepare the bourbon cream sauce to pass around. The sauce is prepared by cooking the eggs, half-and-half, and sugar in a saucepan on medium heat, whisking constantly for 5 minutes or until 160 degrees on a candy thermometer. Remove from heat and stir in bourbon. Makes about 1½ cups of sauce.

Works great using Keebler Pecan Sandies cookies.

Yield: 8 to 10 servings

Easy Carrot Cake with Cream Cheese Frosting

Cake

2	cups sugar	4 eggs
2	cups flour	1 teaspoon salt
1	(14½ ounce) can sliced	1 teaspoon baking soda
	carrots, drained	1 teaspoon cinnamon
1½	cups vegetable oil	

Frosting

1	stick butter	1 tablespoon vanilla
1	(8 ounce) package	½ teaspoon salt
	cream cheese	1 cup chopped nuts
1	(1 pound) box	
	confectioners' sugar	

Preheat oven to 350 degrees. Sift dry ingredients together in bowl. Beat eggs in separate bowl and add to dry ingredients. Stir well. Add oil and drained carrots. Bake in two layers or Bundt pan at 350 degrees for 50 minutes. Prepare frosting by beating all ingredients except nuts until smooth. Ice cake and place chopped nuts on top.

Yield: 8 to 10 servings

"Miss Foggerty's Cake" by Unknown

As I sat by my
window last
evening,
The letterman
brought unto me
A little gilt-edged
invitation
Saying, "Gilhooley,
come over to tea."
Sure I knew 'twas
the Foggertys
sent it,
So I went for old
friendship's sake,
And the first
thing they gave
me to tackle
Was a slice of Miss
Foggerty's cake.
Miss Martin
wanted to taste it,
But really there
wasn't no use,
For they worked at
it over an hour
And couldn't get
none of it loose.
Till Foggerty went
for a hatchet
And Killey came
in with a saw;

(cont'd on next page)

MJ's Apple Cake

4	cups MacIntosh or Red Delicious apples, peeled, cored and chopped into large chunks (about 6 large apples)	2	teaspoons cinnamon
		1½	teaspoons baking soda
		1	teaspoon salt
		2	teaspoons vanilla
		2	eggs
2	cups sugar	¾	cup apple sauce
2	cups flour	1	cup nuts, chopped (optional)

Preheat oven to 350 degrees. Mix together well the first 6 ingredients. In a separate bowl, mix the vanilla, eggs and apple sauce together and then add to the first mixture and mix again thoroughly. Add nuts, if desired, and mix again. In an 11 x 13 inch baking pan, bake at 350 degrees for about 40 minutes. Serve warm and refrigerate any leftover cake.

Cold, this cake has a bread pudding texture.

Yield: 8 to 10 servings

Ruthie Stevenson's Cuban Cake

2	cups flour	½	cup melted butter
1½	cups sugar	1	cup milk
¾	cup cocoa	2	eggs, beaten
2	teaspoons baking soda	1	teaspoon vanilla
1	teaspoon baking powder	1	cup hot, strong brewed coffee

Preheat oven to 350 degrees. Sift together the first five ingredients. Add the melted butter, milk, beaten eggs, vanilla and mix well. Add the coffee last and fold into mixture. Spoon into greased and floured Bundt pan. Bake at 350 degrees about 50 minutes or until done.

Yield: 8 to 10 servings

"Miss Foggerty's Cake" (continued)

The cake was enough, by the powers,
To paralyze any man's jaw.
"Oh, Gilhooley," she cried, "you're not eating,
Just take another piece for my sake."
"No thanks, Miss Foggerty," says I,
"But I'd like the recipe for that cake."
McNulley was took with the colic,
McFadden complained of his head,
McDoodle fell down on the sofa
And swore that he wished he was dead.
Miss Martin fell down in hysterics,
And there she did wriggle and shake,
While every man swore he was poisoned
By eating Miss Foggerty's cake.

Mother's Beulah Cake

3   cups plain flour, divided   ½   cup vegetable
    into one ½ cup and   shortening (such as
    one 2½ cup portion   Crisco)
1   teaspoon baking powder   6   eggs
1   cup margarine (oleo)   1   cup milk
3   cups sugar   2   teaspoons lemon extract

*ℒib Fearing
tells us that her
mother made this
cake so often and it
turned out perfect
every time. "Mother
won several blue
ribbons and prizes
for this cake's
texture and flavor.
She believed the
cake's real success
was her oven. She
got a new stove
and later swore
that the cakes
baked in it were
never the same."*

Preheat oven to 325 degrees. Mix ½ cup flour and the baking powder together and set aside. In a separate bowl, cream margarine, sugar and shortening together, then add eggs, one at a time, beating well with each addition. Add to this mixture, alternately, the remaining 2½ cups flour, milk and lemon extract. Lastly, add the set aside flour and baking powder mixture to the main mixture and mix. Prepare a 10 inch tube pan by lightly greasing it with shortening and dusting it with flour. Pour in cake batter and bake at 325 degrees for 75 minutes. Invert on a wire rack while still in the pan, and allow it to cool (may use a knife to run around inside edges of tube pan to loosen cake when cooled).

Bake in 9 inch layer cake pans at 375 degrees for 25 minutes or make cupcakes by baking at 350 degrees for 20 minutes (fill cups ½ to ⅔ full).

Yield: 10 to 12 servings or 1½ to 2 dozen cupcakes

Granddaughter's Caramel-Pecan Cheesecake

18 squares of sugar graham crackers, crushed

¼ cup granulated sugar

⅓ cup margarine, melted

1 cup pecan halves

2 (8 ounce) packages cream cheese, softened

½ cup brown sugar, packed lightly

2 teaspoons vanilla extract

2 eggs

¼ cup prepared caramel topping (as for ice cream)

This is a favorite of Louise Fields' granddaughter, Chelsea Heslin, age 6.

Preheat oven to 325 degrees. Mix crushed graham crackers, sugar and margarine. Press into bottom and side of a 9 inch pie plate. Finely chop and toast the pecan halves, then sprinkle them evenly on the bottom of the pie crust and set aside. Blend in a bowl the cream cheese, brown sugar and vanilla with a mixer until creamy. Blend in eggs until smooth. Pour into prepared pie crust. Decorate top in a circle with any remaining pecan halves. Bake at 325 degrees for 40 to 45 minutes. Cool on a wire rack at least 4 hours. Before serving, drizzle caramel topping over cheesecake.

Yield: 8 servings

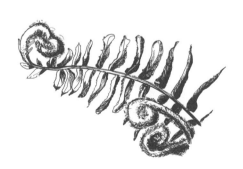

DeBlieu Family Coffeecake or Anne's Sour Cream Coffeecake

Cake

1 cup white (granulated) sugar	2 cups flour
½ cup butter	½ teaspoon salt
2 eggs	1 teaspoon baking soda
1 teaspoon vanilla	1 cup plain yogurt

Topping

⅓ cup brown sugar	¼ cup white sugar
1 cup chopped nuts or coconut	1 teaspoon cinnamon

Jan DeBlieu tells the story of this recipe: "This was a family staple when growing up, especially Sunday mornings before church. Mother gave me the recipe when I went off to College, but I promptly lost the recipe and forgot all about it for many years. Then last spring a childhood friend sent me a copy of a Boston College cookbook where she was a faculty member and to my great surprise and delight... there was our old family recipe!"

Preheat oven to 350 degrees. Prepare the batter by creaming together the sugar and butter until light and fluffy. Add the eggs one at a time beating with each addition. Add the vanilla and beat again. In a separate bowl, sift together the flour salt, and baking soda. Add the dry ingredients and the yogurt, alternately, to the creamed mixture. Prepare the topping by mixing all ingredients together well. Turn half the batter into a greased and floured 9 x 13 inch baking dish or two 8 inch dishes. Add half the topping. Layer on remaining batter then remaining topping. Bake at 350 degrees for 35 to 40 minutes.

Anne Embrey uses a similar recipe. Try adding a second teaspoon of vanilla and substituting 1 cup light sour cream (not fat free) for the yogurt.

Yield: 12 servings

Sweet Potato Cake

½ cup margarine or butter	¼ teaspoon grounds cloves
1 cup sugar	½ teaspoon ground cinnamon
2 eggs	½ teaspoon ground nutmeg
1 cup sweet potatoes, cooked and mashed	½ teaspoon salt
2 teaspoons baking powder	2 cups all-purpose flour
¼ teaspoon baking soda	½ cup milk
	½ cup nuts, optional

Preheat oven to 400 degrees. Cream together in a bowl the margarine and sugar. One at a time, thoroughly beat in the eggs. Blend in the mashed sweet potatoes and beat until smooth. Set aside. In a separate bowl, sift together the baking powder, baking soda, spices, salt and flour. Mix about half this dry ingredient mixture, slowly, into the egg and sweet potato mixture. Slowly add the milk and blend well. Add remaining dry mixture and mix well. Add nuts, if desired. Bake in two 9 inch layer pans which have been greased and lined with paper, or bake in one 10 x 14 inch baking pan similarly greased and lined. Bake at 400 degrees. Cake is done when cake tester comes out clean from center of the pan, about 25 minutes.

Great as is or iced with caramel frosting. Also good served with a lemon or orange sauce on the side.

Yield: 8 to 10 servings

Never Fail Basic Pie Crust

1¼ cup sifted all-purpose
     flour
     "pinch" of salt
3   tablespoons butter

3   tablespoons shortening
3-4 tablespoons cold water
    wax paper
    pie pan, 9-inch

Sift together flour and salt. Cut butter and shortening into flour with pastry blender or knife until mix resembles a coarse meal. Add water and mix with fork then, using finger tips, gather dough into a ball. If dough is very crumbly, sprinkle with water only enough to make dough stick together. Wrap in wax paper and chill in refrigerator at least one hour before rolling out.

Yield: 1 (9-inch) prepared pie crust

We cannot love God unless we love each other, and to love each other we must know each other in the breaking of bread. Heaven is a banquet and life is a banquet, too, even with a crust, where there is companionship. Love comes with community.

Dorothy Day.

Rhubarb Crunch Pie

Filling
3   cups diced (¼ inch
     pieces) young rhubarb
1   cup sugar

2   tablespoons cornstarch
¼   cup water
1   teaspoon vanilla

Crust
2   cups oatmeal
1   cup brown sugar
1   cup margarine

½   cup walnuts (may use
     1 full cup if desired)
1½ cup flour
½   teaspoon baking soda

Preheat oven to 375 degrees. Mix filling ingredients in medium saucepan and cook over low heat until thickened. Prepare crust by mixing all ingredients and placing ¾ of the mixture in a greased 9 x 13 x 2 inch baking dish and pat down to all sides of pan. Pour filling into crust. Crumble remaining crust mix over top. Bake at 375 degrees for 30 minutes.

Yield: 8 servings

Apple Sour Cream Pie

Pie Filling

1	cup sour cream
1	egg
2	teaspoons lemon juice
2	tablespoons flour

3	cups sliced apples (or put apple slices into a 9 inch pie dish until apples well mound above the rim)
1	prepared pie crust

Streusel Topping

⅓	cup sugar
⅓	cup flour

1	teaspoon cinnamon
½	cup butter, cold and hard

Preheat oven to 375 degrees. Combine sour cream, eggs, lemon juice and flour. Fold in sliced apples. Place mixture in prepared pie shell. Prepare streusel in separate bowl by sifting together the dry ingredients. Next in very small pieces, cut the cold butter into the mixture with a knife and mix with a fork. When streusel is "mealy" sprinkle on top of apples (don't worry if instead of "mealy" it turns out sticky; just spread it on top as best you can). Bake at 375 degrees for one hour.

Yield: 6 to 8 servings

This pie won Bruce Nolin a first place in a baking contest in Virginia. "I do one for every major holiday alternating it with my Pumpkin Cheesecake Pie (also found in this cook book), which won second place in the same contest. I was the only male competitor in the contest!"

Grandmother Affie's Pecan Pie

6	eggs
3	cups sugar
1	(12 ounce) can evaporated milk

3	teaspoons vanilla
½	pound butter, melted
4	cups pecans, chopped
3	prepared pie crusts

Preheat oven to 350 degrees. Combine all ingredients. Divide evenly among 3 pie shells. Bake 30-40 minutes at 350 degrees or until crust browns.

Yield: 3 pies

Joyce Pickrel says "This recipe is an old one from my Alexander family cookbook."

Virginia Sweet Potato Pie

2	cups baked, mashed sweet potatoes	½	teaspoon vanilla
1	cup granulated, white sugar	¼	teaspoon cinnamon
		¼	teaspoon ground allspice
2	eggs	⅛	teaspoon ground nutmeg
4	ounces butter, softened to room temperature		milk
		1	prepared pie crust

Lou Overman adds: "This recipe originated in the family four generations ago in Antebellum Southern Virginia. A personal favorite."

Preheat oven to 400 degrees. Mash potatoes thoroughly and beat in sugar. Add eggs and beat again. Add butter and beat again. Add vanilla and spices and beat again. Add only enough milk to soften in order "to pour" into pie shell (consistency of a pumpkin pie batter), beating again until fluffy. Pour into pie shell and bake at 400 degrees for about 30 minutes until center is set to the consistency of custard. Best Served warm with whipped cream but may be served cool.

Add the milk slowly, a little at a time, until about the consistency of a pumpkin pie batter. Be careful since the "wetness" of the sweet potatoes used may vary and you do not want it to be "soupy" as a result.

Yield: 8 servings

Vinegar Pie

3	sticks margarine	3	teaspoons flour
9	eggs	3	teaspoons vanilla
3¾	cups sugar	9	tablespoons milk
6	tablespoons vinegar	2	prepared pie crusts

A Church Social regular, this custard style pie is a long-time favorite in Eastern North Carolina. Ingredients are plentiful and the recipe is easy to make.

Preheat oven to 350 degrees. Melt margarine separately. Beat the eggs smooth in a bowl. Place melted margarine in a bowl and add sugar, then add eggs to margarine. Add vinegar, flour and vanilla. Add milk. Beat until fluffy. Pour into pie shells. Bake at 350 degrees until center is set or does not "jiggle."

Yield: 16 servings

Grape Hull Pie

3 eggs	½ stick margarine, melted
1 cup grape hull preserves (found elsewhere in this cookbook)	1 prepared pie crust

Preheat oven to 375 degrees. Beat the eggs smooth with a fork. Add grape hull preserved (found elsewhere in this cookbook) and melted margarine. Pour into pie shell. Bake at 375 degrees until mixture is set and center does not "jiggle," about 25 to 30 minutes.

Cover pie shell rim with aluminum foil if rim is browning too quickly.

Yield: 6 to 8 servings

"This was a favorite Christmas tradition in the Lou Overman family."

Louise Swain's Lemon Pie

1 (9 inch) prepared deep dish pie shell	1 (14 ounce) can condensed milk
3 eggs, yolks and whites separated	7 teaspoons sugar
⅔ cup lemon juice	¼ teaspoon cream of tartar
	1 teaspoon vanilla extract

Bake pie shell according to package directions. Preheat oven to 350 degrees. Blend egg yolks, lemon juice and condensed milk. Spoon into cooled, baked pie shell. Beat egg whites in a separate bowl. Before they become stiff, add sugar, cream of tartar and vanilla, in that order, one at a time as you beat. Beat until stiff peaks form. Spoon on top of pie and bake in center of oven for about 20 minutes or until top is light to medium brown.

Yield: 6 to 8 servings

Lydia Shimer's Shoofly Pie (Circa 1885)

3 cups flour	1 egg
1 cup granulated sugar	1 (9 inch) prepared pie
½ cup shortening	shell
½ teaspoon salt	1 cup water
1 cup dark molasses	1 teaspoon baking soda

This more than a century old family recipe is a favorite of the Brassington clan.

Preheat oven to 450 degrees. In a bowl, combine the first four ingredients using a fork, two knives or a crumb maker to make a crumb mixture. In a second bowl, beat together the molasses and egg. Add to this the water and baking soda. Put ⅓ of the crumb mixture in the bottom of the unbaked pie shell. Spoon in ½ the molasses mixture. Layer with a second ⅓ crumbs, then remaining molasses mixture. Top with last ⅓ crumb mixture. Bake at 450 degrees for 10 minutes and then reduce heat to 400 degrees. Continue baking for another 20 to 30 minutes.

Yield: 6 to 8 servings

Mocha Pie

½ cup sugar	1 tablespoon cornstarch
1 ounce unsweetened	1 cup milk
baking chocolate	¼ teaspoon salt
1 tablespoon instant	1 teaspoon vanilla
coffee powder	1 cup whipping cream
3 tablespoons flour	1 (8 inch) prepared pie
	shell, baked

Betsy Steketee's story behind this recipe is that "The recipe was my grandmother's. She gave it to me as one of about a dozen favorite family recipe's that have withstood the passage of time as a special wedding gift upon my marriage in 1972."

Cook together the first seven ingredients, stirring constantly, until it thickens. It will thicken quickly. Remove from heat and cool. Stir in vanilla. In a separate bowl, whip cream until stiff. Fold ⅔ of the whipped cream into the cooled chocolate mixture. Partially fold remaining ⅓ whipped cream in for a marbled effect. Pour into baked pie shell and refrigerate.

Can be made a day ahead.

Yield: 6 to 8 servings

Boston Cream Pie

Cake

1 box Duncan Hines
   yellow cake mix

1½ cups orange juice

Filling

1 (3 ounce) box French
   vanilla instant
   pudding

1 cup milk
1 cup whipping cream
1 teaspoon vanilla extract

Icing

3 tablespoons butter
1 tablespoon milk
1 square unsweetened
   chocolate baking bar

1 square semisweet
   chocolate baking bar
½ pound 10X powdered
   sugar
½ teaspoon vanilla extract

Margaret Harvey tells us that for two generations this has been a favorite family dessert. Although originally made from scratch, this simpler recipe is just as good.

Follow box directions for making a two layer cake but substitute orange juice in place of liquid called for by box directions. When cake has cooled, split one layer to make two thinner layers. You may freeze the other full layer for later use or double the filling and icing recipe above to make a second Boston Cream Pie. Mix pudding, milk, whipping cream, and vanilla with an electric mixer for a minute or two until thickened for spreading. Spread between the split layer cake. Prepare icing by melting together over low heat all icing ingredients except the vanilla. When melted, beat until smooth, then add vanilla. Spread over top of cake and refrigerate.

If icing is too thick, add a little more milk until spreading consistency is reached.

Yield: 6 to 8 servings

Best Bourbon Pie

4	eggs, yolks and whites separated	1	envelope gelatin (such as Knox)
½	cup sugar	½	cup bourbon
1	pinch salt	⅓	cup sugar
⅔	cup milk	1	(9 inch) pie crust, baked
¼	cup cold water		

Beat egg yolks with ½ cup sugar. Add salt and milk. Cook in double boiler until of custard consistency and let cool. In the water, dissolve the gelatin and add it to the mixture. Add the bourbon and stir. In a separate bowl, beat egg whites until stiff. Add ⅓ cup sugar and beat. Mix the custard and egg white mixture together and pour into baked pie shell. Refrigerate for 2 to 3 hours. Serve with whipped cream or topping.

Yield: 6 to 8 servings

Sonoma Cobbler

1	(20 ounce) can crushed pineapple, undrained	1	(13 ounce) package (or 1¾ cup) yellow cake mix
1	(16 ounce) package frozen or fresh blueberries, divided into two portions	½	cup pecans, chopped
		¼	cup sugar
		1	stick butter, melted

Preheat oven to 350 degrees. In a 9 x 13 inch oven safe dish, spread the pineapple. Place one portion (half) the blueberries on top of the pineapple; sprinkle over this all the cake mix, then a second layer of the blueberries. Layer on nuts, sugar and pour melted butter over all. Bake at 350 degrees for 35 to 45 minutes.

Yield: 8 servings

Individual French Apple Tarts

Pastry

3   sticks (24 tablespoons) unsalted butter, chilled

3   cups all-purpose flour

4   tablespoons granulated sugar

4   tablespoons ice water

Filling

6   firm, small to medium Granny Smith or MacIntosh apples

⅓   cup sugar

ground cinnamon, to taste

⅓   cup pure apple jelly

Special items

24 foil baking cups

muffin tins for 24 baking cups

On a cold, clean surface, cut the 3 sticks chilled butter into halves, then quarters, then eighths to make 96 butter cubes. In a bowl, combine 3 cups flour and 4 tablespoons sugar. Add the butter cubes to coat each cube with the flour and sugar mixture. Add 4 tablespoons ice water to this and mix or gently toss until the water is absorbed. With warm hands, mix thoroughly so that all the flour and sugar is incorporated and the butter cubes are no longer visible and a ball of dough results. Do NOT use softened butter. Wrap the dough ball in plastic wrap and refrigerate 15 minutes. While dough is chilling, peel, quarter and core the 6 apples so there are 24 quarter sections. Slice each quarter thinly into several wedge shaped slices being sure to set them aside in 24 filling portions. Line the muffin tins with the foil baking cups. Now take the chilled dough and divide it in half and create two 12 inch long pastry logs. Each log is now sliced into twelve 1 inch slices of dough. Place one dough slice in each foil cup and press with fingers to form a pastry "nest" for the apples. Place apple portions with the wedge slices "sharp" edge down into the nests. Sprinkle all 24 tarts with ⅓ cup sugar and cinnamon. Bake in a preheated 350 to 375 degree oven until pastry edges are dark golden brown. Immediately upon removing tarts from oven, use a spoon to remove the tarts in their baking foil cups from the tins (otherwise you will have the apple juices and sugar caramelize and the baking cups will stick to the muffin tins). Melt the apple jelly and glaze each slightly cooled tart with it.

Best served warm with vanilla ice cream.

Yield: 24 tarts

An original recipe for a large pie-sized tart appeared in the Sunday New York Times many years ago and was adapted by Allen W. Wood and first published in the first Habitat for Humanity Cookbook as "French Apple HabiTARTS for Humanity." Allen says, "This is a favorite at all St Andrew's by-the-Sea bake sales and functions." Just ask Rev. Gill for an endorsement.

Best Sugar Cookies from the US and Canada

1	cup butter (2 sticks)	2	eggs
1	cup oil	1	teaspoon vanilla extract
1	cup confectioners' sugar	4½	cups flour
1	cup granulated sugar	1	teaspoon baking soda
		1	teaspoon salt
		1	teaspoon cream of tartar

Preheat oven to 350 degrees. Cream butter, oil and sugars. Add eggs and vanilla. Beat until light and fluffy. In a separate bowl, sift together flour, baking soda, salt and cream of tartar. Blend dry ingredients thoroughly into first mixture. Dough will be sticky. For drop-type cookies, roll into marble size balls with fingers and press flat onto a greased cookie sheet with fingertips. Bake at 350 degrees for 6 to 8 minutes. For fancy cut-shaped cookies, add flour to the dough by "dusting" and kneading until it reaches a consistency for rolling out. Chill covered for at least one hour. Roll flat on wax paper and cut shapes with cookie cutters. Place shaped cookies on greased cookie sheet and bake at 350 degrees for 6 to 8 minutes. Decorate with colored sugar sprinkles before baking, or frost after baking.

Some of our cooks use 5 cups of sugar and bake at 375 degrees. May also add other extracts in addition to vanilla, such as almond or lemon.

Watch closely! Cookies are done when edges are lightly browned!

Yield: 5 dozen

Luelen's Easy Cookies

½ cup butter	1 cup flour
3 ounces cream cheese	½ cup pecans
1 cup sugar	

Preheat oven to 350 degrees. Soften butter and cream cheese together in a blender bowl. Add rest of ingredients, one at a time in order given above, blending after each addition. Drop by spoonfuls onto an ungreased cookie sheet and bake at 350 degrees for 10 minutes.

Yield: 4 dozen cookies (depending on size of "drops")

A mother is one who understands that baking cookies is more important than washing windows.

Unknown.

Split Seconds

2 cups flour	¾ cup (or 1½ sticks) butter, soft or softened
⅔ cup sugar	1 unbeaten egg
½ teaspoon baking powder	2 teaspoons vanilla
	strawberry jelly or jam

Preheat oven to 350 degrees. Sift together flour, sugar and baking powder. Blend in butter, egg and vanilla. Form a dough and divide into 4 parts. Shape each part into a roll about 13 inches long and ¾ inch in diameter. Place the rolls on ungreased cookie sheets about 4 inches apart and two inches from edge of sheet, two rolls per cookie sheet. With the back of a knife, make a depression about ¼ inch deep lengthwise down the center of each roll. Fill the depression with jelly or jam. Bake at 350 degrees for 15 to 20 minutes. While warm, cut diagonally into bars.

Yield: 4 dozen

Very Best Chocolate Chip Cookies

1   cup (2 sticks) butter or margarine at room temperature
¾   cup white granulated sugar
¾   cup brown sugar, packed tightly
2   eggs
2   teaspoons vanilla

2¼ cups unsifted flour
1   teaspoon baking soda
½   teaspoon salt
1   cup chopped nuts (pecans or peanuts are good), optional
2   cups semisweet chocolate chips

Preheat oven to 375 degrees. Cream butter with sugars, eggs and vanilla. In a separate bowl mix together the flour, baking soda and salt. Gradually blend the dry mixture into the creamed mixture. Stir in nuts, if desired, and chocolate chips. Drop by teaspoon onto greased cookie sheets and bake at 375 degrees for 9 to 11 minutes or until golden brown.

For a festive look, use M&M's in place of chocolate chips. For non chocolate eaters who like peanut butter, try using Reese's Pieces in place of the chocolate chips or for those who love both, use a mixture of M&M's and Reese's Pieces.

Yield: 5 dozen

No Bake Tropical Cookies

½   cup peanut butter
½   cup Karo syrup

½   cup brown sugar
3   cups Special K cereal

Mix and place in buttered, square pan. Chill and slice into squares or bars.

If you like these, try adding chocolate chips, nuts or other goodies.

Yield: 16 bars

Excellent treat to make with small children as cook's helpers or to make for themselves with supervision. So easy and quick and absolutely no cooking required.

Crispy Cookies

1 cup white granulated sugar	½ cup nuts, chopped
1 cup brown sugar	3½ cups flour
1 cup margarine	1 teaspoon vanilla
1 cup vegetable oil	1 teaspoon salt
1 large egg	1 teaspoon cream of tartar
1 cup oatmeal	1 cup Rice Krispies Cereal
1 cup coconut	

Preheat oven to 350 degrees. Mix sugars, margarine, oil and egg thoroughly so that oil does not separate. Add the remaining ingredients while stirring and be sure the Rice Krispies are last. Roll into balls and flatten with a fork. Bake at 350 degrees for 10 to 12 minutes.

Yield: 4 dozen

Pumpkin Snack Squares

1 cup flour	⅔ cup cooked pumpkin
1 cup brown sugar	½ cup margarine
1 teaspoon baking powder	2 eggs, beaten
1 teaspoon cinnamon	1 cup miniature chocolate chips

Preheat oven to 350 degrees. Mix first four ingredients in a large bowl. Add the next three ingredients and beat until smooth. Stir in chocolate chips. Pour mixture into a greased 9 x 13 inch baking pan. Bake for 30 minutes. Cool and cut into 2 inch squares.

Yield: 24 brownies

Eat honey, my son, for it is good; honey from the comb is sweet to your taste. Know also that wisdom is sweet to your soul, if you find it, there is a future hope for you, and your hope will not be cut off.

Proverbs 24: 13-14

Butterscotch Brownies

½ cup melted butter
2 cups dark brown sugar
2 eggs
1½ cups flour

2 teaspoons baking powder
1 teaspoon vanilla

Preheat oven to 375 degrees. Grease a 9 inch baking dish with butter. In a bowl, mix all the ingredients together, combining them well. Spread the mixture into the baking dish and bake at 375 degrees for 35 to 40 minutes or until dry on the top and almost firm to the touch. Let cool 10 to 15 minutes before cutting into 2 inch squares.

Yield: 16 brownies

Bourbon Nut Creams

1 pound box extra fine powdered sugar
1 stick real butter
2 ½ ounces bourbon

1½ cups pecans, chopped fine
5 squares bitter chocolate

Cecilia Anne Hill says, "You can't eat just one."

Reserve ½ cup of the sugar. Soften butter, beat and while beating, gradually add the non-reserved sugar. Near the end of adding the sugar, also add the bourbon and pecans a little at a time and alternately. When thoroughly mixed, chill for 1 hour. Remove from refrigerator, roll into balls the size of large marbles and roll into the reserved sugar, using up the sugar. Chill again. Melt the chocolate squares in a bowl over simmering water. With a two tined fork (or other, but two-tined works best), hold each ball and dip the ball into the melted chocolate. Put on wax paper and return to refrigerator. If chocolate runs off, it is too hot, so cool it until it reaches a thickness to stick to the balls. Store in refrigerator.

Yield: 18 candies

Irish Potato Fudge

3 tablespoons butter	1 pound 10X sugar, sifted
3 (1 ounce) squares unsweetened chocolate	1 teaspoon vanilla
	⅛ teaspoon salt
⅓ cup Irish potatoes, cooked, mashed and unseasoned	½ cup nuts, chopped

In a double boiler on simmer, melt the butter and chocolate. Remove from heat and stir in the potatoes. Gradually add the sugar, vanilla and salt, and mix thoroughly. Add nuts. Turn out on a lightly sugared flat surface (sugared with 10 X sugar), and knead until smooth. In an 8 inch buttered dish, press the fudge mix into the bottom and cool in the refrigerator. Cut into small squares. Store dry and cool.

Yield: 16 pieces

Microwave Peanut Brittle

1 cup sugar	⅛ teaspoon salt
½ cup light corn syrup	1 teaspoon butter
1 cup raw peanuts (uncooked), shells removed	1 teaspoon vanilla
	1 teaspoon baking soda

Mix sugar, corn syrup, peanuts and salt together in a large bowl and microwave on high for 8 minutes, stirring halfway through. Carefully add butter and vanilla to hot mixture and mix well. Microwave on high another 1 to 2 minutes or more until peanuts are lightly brown. Use caution - syrup will be very, very hot. Remove from microwave and gently add in and stir the baking soda until light and foamy. Quickly pour onto a lightly buttered cookie sheet that has a rim. Spread and allow to cool for one hour or more. Break into pieces and store in an airtight container.

Yield: 1 pound of candy

Excerpt from
Nobody Knows
But Mother
by Mary Morrison

How many lunches
for Tommy
and Sam?

Nobody knows
but Mother.

Cookies and apples
and blackberry
jam —

Nobody knows but
Mother.

Nourishing
dainties for every
"sweet tooth,"

Toddling Dottie or
dignified Ruth -

How much love
sweetens the
labor, forsooth?

Nobody knows
but Mother.

Caramel Corn

½ cup butter	1 teaspoon baking soda
1 cup sugar	16 cups popcorn, popped
½ cup light corn syrup	1 cup dry roasted peanuts
1 teaspoon vanilla	

Preheat oven to 250 degrees. Bring butter, sugar and syrup to a boil in a saucepan. Reduce heat to medium and cook for 5 minutes, stirring. Remove from heat and add vanilla and baking soda. Mix then pour over a large bowl containing the popped popcorn and roasted peanuts. Put mixture on a large, rimmed cookie sheet and stir well. Bake at 250 degrees for about 1 hour while stirring every 15 minutes. Let cool and store in airtight containers.

Yield: 16 cups or 2 (2-quart) storage containers

Let them give thanks to the Lord for his unfailing love and his wonderful deeds for men, for he satisfies the thirsty and fills the hungry with good things.

Psalm 107: 8-9.

Yogurt Health Bars

2½ cups Grape Nuts cereal	1 cup fresh or dried fruit cut into small pieces
3 tablespoons honey	
2 (8 ounce) containers fruit yogurt (your choice)	⅔ cup nonfat dry milk powder

Spray an 8 inch square pan with vegetable cooking spray. Place ¾ cup Grape Nuts cereal (about ⅓ of total called for in recipe) evenly spread in bottom of pan. In blender, combine honey, yogurt, fruit and milk powder, blending until smooth. Fold in about one half the remaining Grape Nuts cereal and then pour the mixture into the prepared pan. Sprinkle top with the final part of the Grape Nuts cereal. Freeze for at least 4 hours. Cut into 6 to 8 bars and keep in freezer (they will look like ice cream bars).

Yield: 6 to 8 bars

Orange Ice

1½ cups sugar
¾ cup white syrup (such as Karo White Syrup)

1¾ cup water
6 tablespoons lemon juice
3 cups orange juice

Cook sugar, corn syrup and one cup of water (reserving the other ¾ cup of water) until clear on medium heat (doesn't take long). Add lemon and orange juices and the remaining water. Cool and then freeze. Before serving allow to slightly thaw.

Yield: 12 to 14 half cup servings

From Rev Gill's mothers' childhood. This is a light dessert or wonderful pick-me-up for hot weather, true Southern "sittin'-on-the-porch" hospitality.

Burgundy Parfait for Ice Cream

1 (16 ounce) bottle white syrup (such as Karo)
1½ cups white granulated sugar

4-5 drops red food coloring
½ bottle port wine

In a saucepan, bring first three ingredients to a boil. Add the wine and allow to cool Serve in parfait glasses over vanilla or chocolate chip ice cream.

Yield: 8 to 10 servings

An easy to prepare, yet elegant dessert.

Lemon Bisque

1 (12 ounce) can evaporated milk
1 (3 ounce) package lemon gelatin
1¼ cup boiling water

½ cup sugar
⅛ teaspoon salt
3 tablespoons lemon juice
1 (12 ounce) package vanilla wafers

A very good dessert to follow any heavy meal, and a real treat in hot weather.

Chill the milk thoroughly (the colder the milk the more volume produced when whipped) in a bowl in the refrigerator. Let it remain in the refrigerator until the last minute. Crush the vanilla wafers into crumbs and line a 9 x 12 inch pan with these crumbs. To start mixture, dissolve the lemon gelatin in the boiling water. Add the sugar, salt, lemon juice, and stir. When mixture is slightly congealed, beat until thick. Beat the cold milk. Mix the gelatin mixture and milk mixture together. Pour or spoon this final mixture over the crushed wafers and let chill 3 to 5 hours.

Yield: 10 to 12 servings

Cranberry Fool

1 pint heavy (whipping) cream
1 cup white granulated sugar
2 cups cranberries

2 tablespoons confectioners' sugar
juice of 1 lime
4 ounces sour cream

Served with a garnish of extra whipped cream and a thin slice of lime sprinkled with sugar in a champagne or cocktail glass makes this a truly elegant yet easy and light dessert.

Beat heavy cream and granulated sugar until quite firm and stands in peaks. Purée the cranberries, confectioners' sugar, lime juice and sour cream together in a processor or blender. Gently but thoroughly fold the whipped cream into the purée. Refrigerate for 1 to 2 hours until set.

Yield: 6 servings

Kiwi Cloud

5 kiwi fruit	1 cup non-fat frozen
2 teaspoons cornstarch	whipped topping,
1 tablespoon water	thawed
½ cup sugar	kiwi slices, optional,
	garnish

Peel kiwi fruit and purée in a blender (should yield ¼ cup). Dissolve the cornstarch in the water. In a small saucepan, place ½ the kiwi purée, the sugar and the dissolved cornstarch in water. Over medium to low heat, simmer until thickened, about 4 to 5 minutes. Transfer mixture to a bowl and allow to cool. Stir in remaining kiwi purée and chill in refrigerator. When well chilled, fold in the thawed whipped topping. Place in four individual serving dishes and chill until set, about 3 hours. Garnish with kiwi slices, if desired.

Yield: 4 servings

To God who gives our daily bread, a thankful song we raise, and pray that he who sends us food may fill our hearts with praise.

Thomas Talli, 1505–1585.

Toasty Apple-Rice Pudding

⅓ cup maple syrup	2 apples, cored, peeled
2 tablespoons butter	and chopped
¼ teaspoon ground	2 cups cooked rice
cinnamon	2 cups milk
⅛ teaspoon ground	⅔ cup raisins
nutmeg	⅓ cup toasted wheat germ,
	optional

In a medium saucepan, heat syrup, butter, cinnamon, nutmeg and apples until bubbly hot. Add cooked rice, milk and raisins and heat until mixture bubbles again but does not reach a full boil. Reduce heat and simmer, stirring occasionally, until pudding thickens, about 15 minutes. Sprinkle with toasted wheat germ, if desired, and serve.

Yield: 4 servings

For rosy apples, juicy plums, and honey from the bees, we thank you, heavenly Father God, for such good gifts as these.

Unknown.

Summer Fruit Trifle

12 ounces cream cheese, room temperature

½ cup sugar

2 cups chilled whipping cream

2 teaspoons vanilla

4 nectarines, peeled and thinly sliced

1 pint blueberries, washed and cleaned of stems

2 tablespoons additional sugar

1 teaspoon cinnamon

3 tablespoons dark rum

6 tablespoons apricot jam

12 ounces pound cake

Beat cream cheese and ½ cup sugar in a large bowl until light. Gradually beat in cream. Add vanilla and beat until medium-stiff peaks form. Remove ⅔ cup of this cream cheese mixture and reserve in the refrigerator for use as trim. In a separate bowl, combine the fruit, the 2 added tablespoons of sugar, and cinnamon. In a third bowl, mix the rum and jam. Cut the pound cake into ½ inch thick slices. Arrange cake slices in bottom of a deep glass bowl to cover the bowl's bottom. Brush top of cake layer with 3 tablespoons of the jam and rum mixture. Layer over this 2 cups of the fruit mixture. Top with half the cream cheese mixture. Cover this with a second layer of cake, repeat with 3 tablespoons of the jam and rum mix and the 2 cups of fruit layers. Top with remaining cream cheese mixture. Cover this with a third layer of cake. Brush with remaining jam and rum mix, layer on remaining fruit. Cover and chill at least 3 hours or maximum of 8 hours. Before serving use the reserved cream cheese mixture to decorate edges of trifle by spooning it on or piping using a pastry bag.

Yield: 12 servings

Chocolate Delight

Crust

1 cup all-purpose flour	½ cup walnuts, chopped
4 ounces margarine	fine
2 tablespoons granulated sugar	

First Layer

8 ounces cream cheese	1 cup Cool Whip
1 cup 10X sugar	

Second Layer

1 (3 ounce) package instant chocolate pudding	1 (3 ounce) package instant vanilla pudding
	3 cups cold milk
	Cool Whip

Prepare crust by mixing all crust ingredients together and pressing into the bottom of a 9 x 13 inch pan. Prepare first layer by mixing all first layer ingredients and beating until creamy. Spread on crust. Prepare second layer by mixing the two puddings with the milk until it starts to thicken, then pour or spoon onto top of first layer. Top over all with a layer of Cool Whip. Cover with plastic wrap and refrigerate until served. Serve within 6 to 8 hours (Caution - keeps one day only).

Yield: 8 servings

Holiday Memories

Specialty Foods and Just for Fun Treats

Wil Payne

Keep Your Fork

"Seek not outside yourself,
heaven is within."

–Mary Lou Cook

There was a woman who had been diagnosed with a terminal illness and was given only 3 months to live. As she began getting her things "in order," she called her pastor and asked him to come to her house to discuss her final wishes. One of her requests was to be buried with her favorite Bible in her left hand and a fork in her right. The woman explained, "In all my years of attending church socials and potluck dinners, I remember that when the dishes were being cleared, someone would lean over to me and say, 'keep your fork.' It was my favorite part of the meal because I always knew something better was coming, like velvety chocolate cake or deep dish apple pie. I just want people to see me in the casket with a fork in my hand and wonder. Then I want you to tell them, 'keep your fork,' the best is yet to come." The pastor hugged the woman goodbye, knowing it would probably be the last time he would see her, but also understanding that she had a better grasp of Heaven than he did. At the funeral, everyone that walked by the casket saw the fork and asked what it meant. During the pastor's message to the congregation, he explained about the fork and what it symbolized. That fork and its meaning had quite an impact on everyone and they are still sharing the story with people they meet. And now it has been shared with you, so the next time you reach for your fork, let it remind you, oh so gently, that the best is yet to come.

All Occasion Scripture Cake

4½ cups I Kings 4:22	1½ cups Judges 5:25
2 cups Jeremiah 6:20	2 cups I Samuel 30:12
2 cups Nahum 3:12	1 cup Numbers 17:8
2 tablespoons I Samuel 14:25	6 ounces Jeremiah 17:11
½ cup Judges 4:19	1 Leviticus, pinch of Chronicles 9:9, to taste
1 teaspoon Amos 4:5	

Mix thoroughly and place in a greased pan. Bake warmly and share often.

Yield: beyond understanding

A very old, old recipe, originator lost in history.

Liptauer Cheese

½ cup salted butter, softened	1 teaspoon pickled capers, drained
4 ounces cream cheese softened	1 boned anchovy fillet
1 teaspoon (heaping) caraway seeds	1 teaspoon (heaping) Dijon style mustard
	1¼ teaspoons paprika

Cream butter in a small mixing bowl with electric mixer. Add cheese and beat until smooth. Chop caraway seeds in a blender, add capers to the blender and chop. Rinse, dry and chop the anchovy. Add all to creamed cheeses. Add mustard and paprika. Mix well. Shape into desired form and refrigerate until needed.

Yield: 1 cup

Jeanne Pace uses this as a great Christmas gift.

Patriotic Trifle

This red, white and blue dessert is beautiful for any occasion. A light and cool dessert, Kathy Nolin loves to serve it on July Fourth and other patriotic holidays. "I make it with the heavy syrups and whole milk, et al, when feeling decadent and with the fresh fruit and skim milk, et al, when watching calories or fat intake. I like to decorate the top with "flowers" made of reserved thin sliced strawberry petals and a blueberry center. I sometimes use thin kiwi fruit slices for leaves as well."

1 (3 ounce) package vanilla instant pudding, regular or low-fat

2 cups milk, regular or skim

1 angel food cake, cut into 1½ inch thick slices

1 cup blueberries, canned in heavy syrup or fresh and washed with stems removed

1 cup strawberries, canned in heavy syrup or fresh and sliced

1-2 cups Cool Whip, regular or low-fat

In a mixing bowl mix the pudding and milk as directed by package. In a large, clear glass serving bowl, layer in order as follows: angel food cake to completely cover bottom of bowl, half the prepared pudding spread evenly over cake, the blueberries, the remaining cake, remaining pudding, and the strawberries. Top with Cool Whip. Cover with plastic wrap and allow to set several hours or overnight in refrigerator.

Yield: 10 to 12 servings

(Chinese) New Year's Cookies

Gigi Phillip's grandchildren love these easy cookies, and not just at New Year's.

1 (12 ounce) package semisweet chocolate chips

1 (3 ounce) can chow mein noodles

1 cup salted or unsalted peanuts, chopped

Melt chips in double boiler. Mix in noodles and chopped nuts. Drop by teaspoon on wax paper and let set.

Yield: 3 dozen

Easter Story Meringue Cookies

1	cup whole pecans	1	cup sugar
	zipper bags and wooden		electric mixer
	spoons		teaspoons, wax paper,
1	teaspoon vinegar		cookie sheet
	mixing bowl		tape
3	egg whites		Bible
	salt, pinch of		

On Saturday night before Easter Sunday, preheat oven to 300 degrees. Assemble your family in kitchen. Place pecans in zipper storage bags and let children beat them with wooden spoons to break them into small piece. Explain that Jesus was arrested and beaten. Read John 19:1-3. Let each child smell the vinegar. Put 1 teaspoon vinegar into mixing bowl. Explain that Jesus was thirsty on the cross and given vinegar to drink. Read John 19:28-30. Add egg whites to vinegar. Explain that eggs represent life and Jesus gave his life to give us life. Read John 10:10-11. Take a pinch of salt and sprinkle a little on each child's hand to taste, then brush the rest into the bowl. Explain that this represents the tears of Jesus' followers and the bitterness of sin. Read Luke 23:27. Add 1 cup sugar. Explain the sweetest part of the story is that Jesus died because He loved us, wanted us to know this, and belong to Him. Read Psalm 34:8 and John 3:16. Beat with mixer on high for 12 to 15 minutes until peaks are formed. Explain the white color represents that those whose sins are cleansed by Jesus are pure in God's eyes. Read Isaiah 1:18 and John 3:1-3. Fold in the nuts. Drop by teaspoon onto wax paper covered cookie sheet. Explain that each mound represents the tomb where Jesus' body was placed. Read Matthew 27:57-60. Put cookie sheet in oven, close the door and turn the oven off. Give each child a piece of tape to seal the oven door. Explain that Jesus' tomb was sealed. Read Matthew 27:65-66. Tell them they may be sad to leave the cookies in the oven overnight just as Jesus' friends were when the tomb was sealed. Read John 16:20 and 22. Go to bed. Easter morning, open the oven, give each child a cookie, and tell them to take a bite. The cookies are hollow! On the first Easter, Jesus' followers were amazed to find the tomb open and empty. Read Matthew 28:1-9.

Yield: Amazing grace and about 1 dozen cookies

"A Friend's Greeting"
by Edgar A. Guest

I'd like to be the sort
of friend that you
have been to me;
I'd like to be the help
that you've been
always glad to be,
I'd like to mean as
much to you each
minute of the day
As you have meant,
old friend of mine, to
me along the way.
I'd like to do the
big things and
the splendid
things for you,
To brush the gray
from out your
skies and leave
them only blue,
I'd like to say the
kindly thing that I so
oft have heard.
And feel that I
could rouse your
soul the way that
mine you've stirred.
I'd like to give you
back the joy that
you have given me.
Yet that were
wishing you a need I
hope will never be;
I'd like to make you
feel as rich as I,
who travel on

(cont'd on next page)

Festive Chicken (or Turkey) Salad Exotica

1	banana	¼	cup golden raisins
⅓	cup orange juice	¼	cup salted peanuts
4	cups torn greens	½	cup mayonnaise
2	cups cooked chicken or turkey, cubed	½	cup plain yogurt
½	cup jellied cranberry sauce, chilled and cut in ½ inch cubes	1	teaspoon curry powder, or to taste

Slice banana and dip in orange juice. Reserve juice for dressing. Arrange greens in a large bowl. Place banana slices, chicken, cranberry cubes, raisins and peanuts on top of greens and chill. To make dressing, mix reserved orange juice, mayonnaise, yogurt and curry powder in a separate bowl. Pass dressing with the salad and serve with small rolls.

Substitute ½ cup dried cranberries for the jellied cranberry sauce.

Yield: 4 servings

Toasted Pumpkin Seeds for Halloween

1	pumpkin	salt
1	cookie sheet	

Clean out and carve your Jack-o-lantern pumpkin and save the seeds. Wash and clean the seeds. And place them on a cookie sheet. Sprinkle lightly with salt. Bake in a preheated oven at 375 degrees for about 20 minutes, turning or stirring them once or twice while baking.

Yield: 1 cup

Holiday Pumpkin Cheesecake

Crust

6	tablespoons butter
2	cups finely crushed ginger snap cookies

Cheesecake

2	(8 ounce) packages cream cheese
1	cup canned pumpkin or fresh prepared pumpkin
1	cup brown sugar, lightly packed
¼	cup all-purpose flour
1½	teaspoons vanilla
1	teaspoon ground cinnamon
1	teaspoon ground ginger
1	teaspoon ground allspice
½	teaspoon ground nutmeg, optional
½	teaspoon salt
¾	cup milk
4	eggs, slightly beaten

Bruce Nolin's family and in-laws demand this when they get together for Thanksgiving or Christmas.

One to two days before the holiday, preheat oven to 350 degrees. Prepare crust by melting butter and then blending in ginger cookies. Press this mixture into an ungreased 9 or 10 inch pie plate to cover the bottom and sides. Bake at 350 degrees for 10-12 minutes or until edges are well browned. Place aside to cool but leave oven on. Using an electric mixer, beat the cream cheese until smooth. Add pumpkin and brown sugar. Beat 3-5 minutes or until light and fluffy. Beat in flour, vanilla, spices, and salt. Add milk and eggs and beat only until just blended. Pour into prepared, cooled crust and bake at 350 degrees for 75-90 minutes or until knife in center comes out clean. Remove pie and cool on rack for about two hours. Cover with plastic wrap and refrigerate until Thanksgiving or Christmas dinner is done.

Fresh prepared pumpkin: cut off rind and cube pumpkin meat. Boil and mash as you would mashed potatoes (no seasonings). Squeeze or drain off as much excess water as possible. This may be conveniently frozen in 2 cup portions in freezer bags. When thawed, use one cup for the cheesecake and the second one to make pumpkin bread or muffins.

Yield: 8 to 10 servings

Traditional English Egg Nog

6   eggs (separate the yolks   2   quarts light cream or
    and the whites)   half-and-half
1   cup granulated sugar   ½   cup confectioners' sugar
1   pint cognac   nutmeg
1   cup light rum

Carol Brassington says this recipe came from her husband's mother. It has been in the Brassington family a very long time, traditionally drunk before Christmas Mass up north, and brings back many happy memories.

Beat egg yolks until thick. Add granulated sugar, beating until light. Add cognac and rum. Add 1½ quarts cream and ½ the egg whites, beating until well combined. In a separate bowl, beat the remaining egg whites until foamy. Add confectioners' sugar to the egg whites, beating well after each addition. Beat until soft peaks form. Gently stir egg white mixture and remaining ½ quart cream into the egg yolk mixture. Refrigerate. Sprinkle nutmeg on top before serving.

May use 2 cups cognac and no rum.

Yield: 20 (6 ounce) servings

Easiest Egg Nog

1   quart Egg Nog Ice   1   cup light rum, bourbon
    Cream   or brandy
1   cup whole milk   ground nutmeg

Slightly soften ice cream in a punch bowl. Blend in remaining ingredients except nutmeg. Sprinkle top of mixture with nutmeg. Serve.

Recipe easily doubles.

Yield: 8 to 10 (4 ounce punch cup) servings.

Bell and Star Sweet Potato Angel Biscuits

3	packages active dry yeast	1½	cups sugar
¾	cup warm water	1	tablespoon baking powder
3	cups canned sweet potatoes	1	tablespoon salt
7½	cups all-purpose flour	1½	cups shortening

In a two-cup measuring cup, pour the dry yeast into the warm water. Set it aside for 5 minutes. It will foam up like bubble bath. Meanwhile, heat the sweet potatoes in a microwave for 3 minutes, mash them and set aside. In a large mixing bowl, combine flour, sugar, baking powder and salt. Cut into dry ingredients the shortening using a pastry blender or fork until crumbly. Pour in yeast mixture and stir in mashed, warm, sweet potatoes. Place this dough on a floured surface and knead with the lower palm of hands for 5 minutes. Put kneaded dough in a bowl sprayed with cooking spray. Also spray top of dough. Cover with aluminum foil and refrigerate for 8 hours or overnight. Preheat oven to 400 degrees. Again, on a floured surface, roll out dough with a rolling pin to ½ inch thick. Help your children cut bells and stars from dough with cookie cutters. Allow 20 minutes to rise (should double in size) before baking at 400 degrees for 10 to 12 minutes. Serve hot with butter or later with thin sliced ham and honey mustard.

Dough freezes well for up to one month. Thaw for 30 minutes before proceeding with process of rolling out and cutting biscuits.

Yield: 7 dozen

The Davenport family likes to make these ahead of time for parties, especially during the winter holidays when so much entertaining is done, and the whole family becomes involved in cutting out the biscuits. They keep so well that Elizabeth says she has even frozen the cooked biscuits for several months successfully.

Molded Celebration Fruit Salad with Dressing

Makes a very pretty dish for holidays like Christmas. Lee Doran sometimes reverses the flavors of the gelatin for the first and second layers for a varied festive appearance.

Salad First Layer

1 large (29 ounce) can sliced peaches, drained reserving ¾ cup juice
1 (3 ounce) package lemon gelatin

¾ cup hot water
2 tablespoons lemon juice
8-10 maraschino cherries, sliced in half
½ cup walnuts or pecan halves

Salad Second Layer

1 (3 ounce) package lime gelatin
¾ cup hot water
2 tablespoons lemon juice

1 (8 ounce) package cream cheese
1 medium (15¼ ounce) can pears, drained discarding juice

Dressing

1 cup marshmallow cream
1 tablespoon lemon juice

1 tablespoon orange juice
¼ cup mayonnaise

Make first layer by dissolving the lemon gelatin in the hot water, then adding the peach juice and lemon juice. In a 9 x 12 inch dish, place about ⅓ of the mixture and chill until about half set. Arrange peaches, cherries and nuts on top in a decorative pattern. Carefully add remaining Jello on top and chill. Make second layer by dissolving lime gelatin in hot water and adding lemon juice. Place in a blender with cream cheese and blend until smooth. Add pears and blend again. Pour second layer over first layer and chill. To make dressing, whip the first three ingredients, then stir in the mayonnaise. Pass dressing with salad or serve up salad with a dollop of dressing on top.

Yield: 12 servings

Cranberry-Ginger Chutney

1 medium lemon	1 clove garlic, minced
12 ounces fresh cranberries	1 jalapeño pepper, seeded and minced
2 cups sugar	1 cinnamon stick
½ cup crystallized ginger, diced	½ teaspoon dry mustard
⅓ cup onion, finely chopped	½ teaspoon salt

Grate yellow zest of lemon and discard white pith. Cut lemon in half, discard seeds and dice lemon meat into ¼ inch pieces. Combine all ingredients in medium non-reactive (not aluminum; recommend glass, ceramic or porcelain coated) saucepan. Bring contents to a boil over medium heat to dissolve sugar. Reduce heat to low and simmer 10 to 15 minutes until cranberries have burst and sauce is thick. Cool completely, cover tightly and refrigerate. Before serving, remove cinnamon stick and let warm to room temperature.

Wonderful with meat and poultry.

Yield: 3 cups

Wine Jelly

2 cups any sweet or dessert wine	1 packet Sure-Jell or Certo
3 cups granulated white sugar	sealing paraffin

Boil wine and sugar in an overly deep pot until sugar is dissolved (it will boil up fast). Add Certo or Sure-Jell and continue to boil for exactly and only 30 seconds. Remove from heat and skim off the foam that develops as it boils with a metal spoon. Pour into sterilized jelly jars and seal with paraffin.

Yield: 6 (8 ounce) jelly jars

ℒou Overman says that adding green food coloring to Chablis based jelly and adding red food coloring to a sweet Red or Rose wine makes nice Christmas gifts when given in pairs.

Corn Pudding

*Marilyn
O'Bleness'
grandson, Devin
Parsons, made this
"surprise" when he
was 5 years old for
breakfast. It is his
original recipe.
"Papaw must be
special because he
was the only one
who got milk added
to his. When served,
you must, I repeat
must, eat it."*

1   can (any size) whole
    kernel yellow corn

1   small handful Corn
    Chex cereal

    milk, optional

Open the can of corn, do not drain. Put in a bowl. Float a small handful cereal on top. Serve cold. For "Papaw" only, add milk.

Yield: 4 servings or more

Missionaries' Downfall Wassail

1   gallon apple cider

½   teaspoon salt

1   cup granulated sugar or
    honey

24   whole cloves

32   whole allspice

6-8 cinnamon sticks

Combine all ingredients in large pan and bring to a rolling boil. Remove from heat and let cool overnight. Strain. Refrigerate until served. Serve hot with your favorite "spike."

Yield: 24 (6 ounce) servings

Cranberry-Mince Pie

*Marylou
Hogan says this is
a great compromise
if you don't
particularly like
mincemeat and
heavenly if you love
cranberries.*

1   (15 ounce) can whole
    cranberry sauce

1¼ cups mincemeat

1   (9 inch) pie shell,
    unbaked

1   cup pecans or walnuts,
    chopped fine

2   tablespoons sugar

2   tablespoons butter,
    melted

Preheat oven to 425 degrees. Mix cranberry sauce and mincemeat together. Stir well and pour into unbaked pie shell. In a bowl, toss together lightly the nuts, sugar and melted butter. Spread this mixture evenly over the top of the pie filling. Bake at 425 degrees until brown and bubbly, about 35 minutes.

Yield: 6 to 8 servings

Fruitcake Haters' Delight

1 cup (or more) leftover crumbled fruitcake		sherry
	1	quart vanilla ice cream

Let fruitcake soak up enough sherry to fully moisten the cake. Soften the ice cream. Fold the fruitcake and wine mixture into the ice cream. Refreeze.

Yield: 4 to 6 servings

This is a "mix to taste" recipe. JoKitt Vinson likes lots of fruitcake and sherry in her ice cream; others may prefer only a "hint" of the mix.

Fruitcake Cookies

½ cup butter	3 teaspoons baking soda
1 cup brown sugar	1 teaspoon ground cloves
4 eggs	½ teaspoon ground nutmeg
3 cups all-purpose flour, divided into a 2 cup and a 1 cup portion	½ teaspoon ground cinnamon
3 cups pecans	2 ounces whole milk
2 cups raisins	5 ounces orange juice
2 pounds fruit cake commercial fruit mixture	

Preheat oven to 325 degrees. Cream together butter, sugar and finally the eggs. In a separate bowl, mix 1 cup of flour with the pecans, raisins and fruit cake mix. In a third bowl, combine the remaining 2 cups of flour, baking soda, and spices. Add to this third bowl the creamed mixture then add, alternately while stirring, the milk and orange juice. Add fruit and nut cake mixture to batter and blend well. Drop by teaspoon onto greased cookie sheet. Bake at 325 degrees for 12 to 15 minutes.

Yield: 6 dozen

Swedish Nut Gift For Any Occasion

4	cups walnut halves	1	teaspoon vanilla
3	egg whites	½	cup butter
1	cup sugar		

Great in fancy jars for Christmas, hostess, or thank you gifts.

Preheat oven to 325 degrees. Put walnuts on a baking sheet and bake at 325 degrees for 10 to 15 minutes. Remove from oven and cool. Beat egg whites until stiff. Add sugar gradually and beat. Add vanilla slowly and beat. In a 9 x 13 inch baking dish, melt the butter. Dip the nuts into the egg white and sugar mixture to coat each nut and place on top of melted butter in baking dish. When all nuts are coated and in the dish, stir and bake at 325 degrees for 30 minutes, stirring frequently.

Yield: 4½ cups

Party Cha-Cha

Crust and topping

15	graham cracker squares, crushed	2	teaspoons sugar
		½	cup butter melted

Filling

1	pint whipping cream	1	(20 ounce) can cherry pie filling
2	tablespoons sugar		
1	(10 ounce) package miniature marshmallows		

A very pretty red and white dessert by Betsy Steketee, it is a delight at Christmas, Valentine's Day, and any hot summer day with a special or festive occasion.

Combine crust and topping ingredients, mixing well. Reserve ½ cup of this mixture for topping and press remaining amount into a 9 x 13 inch baking dish. Whip the cream with 2 tablespoons sugar until soft peaks form. Fold in marshmallows. Spread half this mixture over the crumb crust. Top with cherry pie filling. Spread remaining cream mixture over pie filling and sprinkle reserved topping over all. Refrigerate until ready to serve.

Yield: 12 servings

Aromatic Christmas Dough Ornaments (for Decoration Only)

2¾ cups all-purpose flour
¾ cups salt
¼ cup ground cinnamon
1 tablespoon ground allspice
1 tablespoon ground cloves

¾ teaspoon powder alum
1¼ cup water
drinking straws, ⅜ inch in diameter
9 inch lengths of ribbon or raffia for hangers

Preheat oven to 250 degrees. Combine first six ingredients in a medium mixing bowl and mix well. Add water and mix thoroughly to form a dough. Shape dough into a ball. Knead ball on a lightly floured flat surface for about 5 minutes or until dough is smooth. If too stiff, sprinkle with water. If too moist, sprinkle with flour. Roll dough out to about ¼ inch thick on lightly floured surface, working a small portion of the dough at one time. Cut shapes with cookie cutters. Near top of cookie cut out, make a hole using the drinking straw for later stringing a hanger through the hole. Place cut out shapes on a vegetable cooking sprayed pie plate or cookie sheet. Bake at 250 degrees for about 2 hours until tops are dry and firm to the touch. Remove ornaments to a rack and set aside for 24 hours to completely dry and harden. Insert ribbon or raffia through hole in top of cut out shape for hanging ornament and knot ends.

May be cooked in microwave oven on 30 percent (medium low) for 5 to 8 minutes or until tops of cut outs feel dry. Rotate plate in microwave and check the ornaments every two minutes until done, then cool on rack and set aside for 24 hours to completely dry. Insert hanger through hole.

Ornaments may be embellished with cinnamon candies, whole cloves, all spice, and small amounts of dough that is moistened with water to secure the dough to the cut out shapes.

Aromatic Christmas Spices

2 cups water	1 whole nutmeg (or 1 teaspoon ground nutmeg)
1 tablespoon whole cloves	
3 cinnamon sticks	

Simmer all ingredients in a medium size pan. Add more water and spices when needed.

Yield: 2 cups

Finger Paint

1 cup liquid starch	2 tablespoons Ivory Snow powdered soap flakes
food coloring	

Mix all ingredients and stir well to make paint.

Great for young people for making unique and festive gift bags from old paper bags, while also helping to recycle these bags for another use.

Kool-Aid Play Dough

A favorite at the St. Andrew's By-the Sea Preschool, the young people love the different colors and smells. It is easy to make, inexpensive, and easier for the kids to roll out and cut with cookie cutters than most commercial play dough.

2 cups self-rising flour	4 tablespoons crème of tartar
2 cups Kool-Aid powder, any flavor or color as desired	2 tablespoons cooking oil
1 cup salt	2 cups boiling water

Sift first four ingredients together in a medium size cooking pot. Add the oil and while stirring constantly and slowly, pour boiling water over ingredients. Place on medium heat until dough separates from pot. This will happen almost immediately. Turn dough out of pot onto a lightly floured surface and knead until smooth. Keep in tightly sealed containers or plastic bags.

Hints and Helps

Helpful Hints, Cooking Tips,
Substitutes and Measures,
Seasonings, Times and Temperatures

Devin Sanders

Recipe for Happiness

*"Perhaps too much of everything
is as bad as too little."*

—Edna Ferber

Take twelve whole months. Clean them thoroughly of all bitterness, hate, and jealousy. Make them just as fresh and clean as possible. Now cut each month into twenty-eight or thirty-one parts, but don't make the whole batch at once. Prepare it one day at a time out of these ingredients. Mix well. Add to each day one part of hope, faithfulness, generosity, meditation, and one good deed. Season the whole batch with a dash of good spirits, a sprinkle of fun, a pinch of play, and a cupful of good humor. Pour all of this into a vessel of love. Cook thoroughly over radiant joy, garnish with a smile, and serve with quietness, unselfishness, and cheerfulness. You're bound to have a happy year.

Household Helps and Hints

Brown crust on roasted chicken — rub skin generously with mayonnaise before cooking.

To thin-slice meats such as for stroganoff — partially freeze meat first so will cut easily.

Leftover egg yolks — add two tablespoons of salad oil; this will keep them from hardening and they will remain fresh for several days.

Removing burned food from oven — place a small cloth saturated with ammonia in the oven overnight, then wipe oven clean.

Eggs crack when boiling — add a little vinegar; this will help seal the egg.

Remove grease from soup — a lettuce leaf dropped into the pot will absorb the grease from the top of homemade soup; discard leaf as soon as it has served its purpose.

Sour fruit cooking — add a pinch of salt; this will reduce the amount of sugar you will need to sweeten them.

Hardened brown sugar — place a piece of apple in with the sugar for a few days.

Prevent browned cauliflower while cooking — add a little milk to the water.

Prevent browning apple and banana slices — dip them immediately in lemon juice to prevent darkening.

To ripen tomatoes — place in brown paper bag in a dark cupboard overnight

To absorb cabbage odor while cooking — place a half cup vinegar on the stove near the cabbage.

Prevent "gluey" noodles and rice — add two teaspoons cooking oil to the water before cooking.

Prevent fat splattering — sprinkle a little salt in the frying pan.

¼ cup shortening — use a regular size ice cream scoop when a recipe asks for this.

Refrigerator maximum storage quality temperature — 36 to 40 degrees

Food storage guide:

Dried fruit and nuts — tightly closed containers at room temperature.

Canned fruits — cool dry place; opened cans may be stored covered in refrigerator.

Flour and cereals — room temperature in tight containers

Dairy products — tightly covered in refrigerator; glass jars are excellent.

Eggs — store refrigerated in original containers; yolks store refrigerated in tightly covered containers for 2 to 3 days; whites store refrigerated in tightly covered containers for 7 to 10 days

Meat — store loosely wrapped in refrigerator; fresh meats prepackaged in moisture-vaporproof wrap can be refrigerated as is for 1 to 2 days; for longer periods loosen wrap at both ends; fresh meats in butcher paper should be re-wrapped loosely in waxed paper; cooked meats should be cooled, covered and refrigerated promptly

Poultry — do not chop or cut fresh poultry until ready to use; remove stuffing and bones from cooked poultry as soon as possible, chill and cover or wrap separately

Fish — store in moisture-vaporproof bags or tightly covered containers in refrigerator

BEEF	Roasts	3 to 5 days
	Steaks	3 to 5 days
	Ground beef or stew meat	2 days
PORK	Roasts	3 to 5 days
	Hams, picnic or whole	7 days
	Bacon	7 to 14 days
	Chops or spare ribs	2 to 3 days
	Sausage	1 to 2 days
VEAL	Roasts	3 to 5 days
	Chops	4 days
LAMB	Roasts	3 to 5 days
	Chops	3 to 5 days
	Ground lamb	2 days
POULTRY	Chickens, whole	1 to 2 days
	Chickens, cut up	2 days
	Turkeys, whole	1 to 2 days
Cooked meats		4 days
Cooked poultry		2 days
Cooked hams, picnic		7 days
Cooked frankfurters		4 to 5 days
Sliced luncheon meats		3 days
Unsliced Bologna		4 to 6 days

Measure Conversions and Ingredient Substitutions

WEIGHTS AND MEASURES:

1 fluid ounce	=	2 tablespoons
3 teaspoons	=	1 tablespoon
4 tablespoons	=	¼ cup
5 ⅓ tablespoons	=	⅓ cup
8 tablespoons	=	½ cup = 1 gill
10 ⅔ tablespoons	=	⅔ cup
12 tablespoons	=	¾ cup
16 tablespoons	=	1 cup
1 cup	=	8 fluid ounces
1 cup	=	½ pint
2 cups	=	1 pint
4 cups	=	1 quart = 32 ounces
4 quarts	=	1 gallon
8 quarts	=	1 peck
4 pecks	=	1 bushel
1 orange (medium)	=	½ cup juice
1 lemon (medium)	=	3 tablespoons juice
28 saltine crackers	=	1 cup fine crumbs
14 graham cracker squares	=	1 cup fine crumbs
22 vanilla wafers	=	1 cup fine crumbs
1 ½ slices bread	=	1 cup soft crumbs
1 slice bread	=	¼ cup dried crumbs

CAN SIZES:

No. 2 Can	=	2 ½ cups or 20 ounces
No. 2 ½ Can	=	3 ½ cups or 29 ounces
No. 3 Cylinder	=	5 3/4 cups or 46 fluid ounces
No. 10 Can	=	12 to 13 cups or 6 pounds 8 ounces to 7 pounds 5 ounces (equal to 7 No. 303 cans or 5 No. 2 cans)
No. 300 Can	=	1 3/4 cups or 14 to 16 ounces
No. 303 Can	=	2 cups or 16 to 17 ounces

Hints and Helps

EMERGENCY SUBSTITUTIONS:

¾ cup cracker crumbs	=	1 cup bread crumbs
1 square chocolate (1 ounce)	=	3 tablespoons cocoa plus 1 tablespoon vegetable shortening
1 cup self-rising flour	=	1 cup all-purpose flour plus ½ teaspoon salt and 1 teaspoon baking powder
1 cup sifted cake flour	=	1 cup sifted all-purpose flour minus 2 tablespoons
2 cups cake flour	=	1¾ cup all-purpose flour
1 teaspoon baking powder	=	¼ teaspoon baking soda plus ½ cup buttermilk or sour milk (to replace ½ cup liquid called for in recipe)
1 teaspoon baking powder	=	¼ teaspoon baking soda plus ½ teaspoon cream of tartar
1 cup powdered sugar	=	1 cup granulated sugar plus 1 teaspoon cornstarch in blender until powdered
½ cup brown sugar	=	2 tablespoons molasses plus ½ cup granulated sugar
⅔ cup honey	=	1 cup sugar plus ⅓ cup water
1½ cups corn syrup	=	1 cup sugar plus ½ cup water
1 tablespoon corn starch (for thickening)	=	2 tablespoons flour or 4 teaspoons quick cooking tapioca
1 cake compressed yeast	=	2 teaspoons active dry yeast
1 cup whole milk	=	½ cup evaporated milk plus ½ cup water or 1 cup reconstituted nonfat dry milk plus 2½ teaspoons butter or margarine
1 cup sweet milk	=	1 cup sour milk plus 1 teaspoon baking powder
1 cup sour milk or buttermilk	=	1 tablespoon lemon juice or vinegar plus sweet milk to make 1 cup; let stand 5 minutes
1 cup raw rice	=	3 cups cooked rice
1 cup oil (for baking)	=	1 cup applesauce
1 cup tomato juice	=	½ cup tomato sauce plus ½ cup water
1 cup catsup or chili sauce	=	1 cup tomato sauce plus ½ cup sugar and 2 tablespoons vinegar (for cooking use only)

Flavoring Foods Without Salt

Salt is highly overrated and many herbs and spices enhance flavor, add zest and make the missing salt less noticeable. In general, experiment. Start with small amounts (¼ teaspoon for four servings) and increase to suit your taste. Don't use more than three herbs in one dish. Protect herb flavor and aroma by storing in cool dry spaces in airtight containers. Overall seasonings and herbs such as onion, garlic, lemon, vinegar, peppers, sugar, parsley, basil, thyme, marjoram, rosemary, oregano, and paprika are excellent and found in most kitchens.

MEASURES:

2 teaspoons chopped fresh herbs	=	½ teaspoon dry form
1 clove garlic	=	⅛ teaspoon garlic powder
1 small fresh onion	=	1 tablespoon instant minced onion, rehydrated
1 teaspoon dry mustard	=	1 tablespoon prepared mustard

MEATS:

BEEF	bay leaf, dry mustard, nutmeg (in ground beef/meat loaf), sage, dill, green pepper, fresh mushrooms or tomatoes.
VEAL	bay leaf, curry, ginger, apricot or current jelly, fresh mushrooms or tomatoes, tarragon, dry mustard
PORK	sage, caraway, nutmeg, apples, applesauce, cranberry sauce, tarragon, dry mustard
LAMB	curry, mint, dill, sage
POULTRY	sage, tarragon, fresh mushrooms, poultry seasoning, curry, peaches, apricots, pineapple, lemon, hot pepper sauce, bay leaf
FISH AND EGGS	dill, basil, tarragon, curry, dry mustard, paprika, cayenne, thyme, green pepper, fresh mushrooms or tomatoes, hot pepper sauce, chives, bay leaf

COOKED VEGETABLES:

ASPARAGUS	lemon, chives
BROCCOLI	lemon, oregano, rosemary
CABBAGE	caraway, dill, basil, rosemary, savory, paprika
CARROTS	lemon, orange, nutmeg, mint, basil, marjoram, oregano, thyme, brown sugar, ginger, cinnamon, mace, anise, dry mustard
CORN	green pepper, fresh tomatoes, paprika, hot pepper sauce
GREEN BEANS	marjoram, nutmeg, dill, thyme, lemon, rosemary, basil
PEAS	mint, dill, fresh mushrooms, basil, marjoram, savory
SPINACH	nutmeg, oregano, basil, marjoram, rosemary, thyme, allspice, mace, lemon
OTHER GREEN VEGETABLES	basil, dill, oregano, lemon, fresh mushrooms
POTATOES	mace, chives, rosemary, dill
SQUASH OR SWEET POTATOES	mace, ginger, basil, cloves, cinnamon, brown sugar, nutmeg, allspice, oregano, lemon, orange
TOMATOES	basil, oregano, thyme, sugar, dill, marjoram, vinegar

SALADS:

VARY the vinegars and oils. Match equal parts flavored vinegar such as raspberry, red-wine, champaign to one part oil such as hazelnut, walnut or olive. Add a little sugar, lemon, salt or pepper if you like.

INCLUDE an exotic vegetable to your usual green salads, such as thin strips of sweet potatoes, enoki mushrooms, chopped raw fennel, hearts of palm or roasted red sweet peppers.

MAKE your salad into a main dish with sardines, sliced pepperoni, deli meat or shrimp. Marinate these for 30 minutes in Italian salad dressing before adding to your salad.

ADD bite-size pieces of unique cheeses such as smoked Swiss, Camembert, fontina, or feta.

SWEETEN salads with fruit such as diced apples, pears, berries, grapes, citrus slices or dried fruits. Use a sweeter dressing such as honey mustard or poppy seed for fruit filled salads.

SEASONING MIXES:

(use for seasoning salads, soups, vegetables, meat, seafood and poultry):

Mix A

2	teaspoons thyme
2½	teaspoons savory
2	teaspoons sage
2	teaspoons rosemary
2½	teaspoons marjoram

Mix B

3	teaspoons thyme
1½	teaspoons sage
2½	teaspoons rosemary
3	teaspoons marjoram

Mix C

2	teaspoons basil
1	teaspoons oregano
2	teaspoons onion powder
½	dried grated lemon peel
⅛	teaspoons ground black pepper
1	celery seed

Temperatures and Cooking Times:

VEGETABLE TIME TABLE:

Vegetable cooking (in minutes)	Boiled	Steamed	Baked
Asparagus, tied in bundles	30	35–40	
Artichokes, French	40	45–60	
Beans, Lima	20–40	60	
Beans, string	15–45	60	
Beets, young with skins on	45	60	70–90
Cabbage, chopped, cut sectional	10–20	25	
Cauliflower, stem down	20–30		
Carrots, cut across	20–30	40	
Chard	60–90	90	
Celery, cut in 1/2 inch lengths	30	45	
Corn, green and tender	5–10	15	20
Cucumbers, peeled and cut	20	30	40
Eggplant, whole	30	40	45
Onions	45	60	60
Parsnips	60	75	75
Peas, green	20–40	35–50	
Peppers	20–30	30	30
Potatoes, depending on size	20–40	60	45–60
Pumpkin, in cubes	30	45	60
Potatoes, sweet	40	40	45–60
Salsify	25	45	
Spinach	20	30	
Squash, in cubes	20–40	50	60
Tomatoes, depending on size	5–15	50	15–20
Turnips, depending on size	30-60		

BAKED OR ROASTED
MEATS AND POULTRY:

	Time per Pound (in minutes)	Temperature
Beef (after searing), rare	10–15	300
Beef (after searing), medium	15–25	300
Beef (after searing), well done	25–30	300
Pork	40–55	350
Ham, smoked	30	300
Lamb (after searing)	30	300
Mutton	35	300
Veal	35	325
Chicken	25	350
Duck	25	350
Turkey, large	20	275
Turkey, small	25	300
Fish	20	375

BROILING (3 to 4 inches from heat) and **PAN BROILING:**   **TIME** (in minutes)

Beef Steaks	1 inch thick	8-14 (rare to medium)
	1½ inches thick	10-18 (rare to medium)
	2 inches thick	18-28 (rare to medium)
Hamburgers	¾ inch thick	10
Pork Chops	thin	8–10
Ham Slices, fully cooked, bone in	½ inch thick	10–12
	1 inch thick	16–20
Lamb Chops or Steaks	thin, rib	6–8
	1 inch thick	12-14 (medium)
	1½ inches thick	18 (medium)
Lamb Loin or Shoulder		8–10
Mutton Chops	1 inch thick	15-20
Veal Cutlets	very thin	6–8
Veal Chops		10

Cake, Pastry, and Other Sweet Baking Tips: What Went Wrong?

CAKES IN GENERAL:

Why did the cake rise unevenly in the oven?

- Flour was not blended sufficiently into the main mixture
- Sides of pan were greased unevenly
- Temperature inside oven was uneven
- Oven temperature was too high

Why did mixture overflow the pan?

- Size of pan recommended by recipe was not used; uncooked mixture should fill the pan by no more than two-thirds

Why is the cake overcooked or the top burned?

- All recipes unless specified are for conventional ovens; if using a convection oven or other non-conventional oven, refer to the manufacturer's manual
- Rich fruit cakes usually require longer baking time so they should be covered with foil halfway through baking

Why is the cake burned on the bottom?

- Poor quality pan was used, usually too thin and developed hot spots and warped in the oven
- Cake baked near the bottom of the oven

Why are there holes in the baked cake?

- Pan with the raw whisked mixture was not rapped on the working surface to remove large air pockets before baking

WHISKED OR SEPARATED EGG MIXTURES:

Why is the cake texture dense and heavy?

- Eggs were too small
- Insufficient air was whisked into egg and sugar mixture
- Flour was not folded in gently by hand with large metal spoon
- Melted butter was too hot when added
- Oven temperature was too low

Why did top of cake drop?

- Oven temperature was too hot
- Cake was not cooked long enough
- Cake pan was bumped during baking
- Oven door was opened too soon creating a draft

Why did the Jelly Roll crack while being rolled?

- Sponge was overcooked and so was too dry
- Mixture was not spread out evenly in the baking tray so some parts overcooked and dried out too soon
- Crisp edges of the cooked sponge were not trimmed away before rolling
- Sponge was left too long before rolling

BLENDED AND CREAMED MIXTURES:

Why did the mixture curdle?

- Ingredients were not at room temperature

- Butter and sugar were not creamed together well enough before adding eggs
- Eggs were added too quickly

Why is the cake texture heavy?

- Butter, sugar and eggs were not beaten together long enough
- Flour was stirred in too vigorously knocking the air from the mixture during creaming
- Too much flour was added to the creamed mixture
- Baking powder was left out
- Oven temperature was not hot enough

Why has cake peaked and cracked?

- Oven temperature was too hot so outside formed a crust too quickly and as cake center continued to rise, it burst up through the cake top
- Cake was on too high a shelf in the oven

Why did the dried fruit sink in the cake?

- Fruit pieces were too large and heavy
- The sugary syrup on the outside of the dried fruit was not washed off, causing the fruit to slide through the mixture when heated
- The washed and dried fruit was not dusted with flour before adding to mixture
- Cake mixture was over-beaten or too wet so it could not hold up the fruit
- Oven temperature was too low

PASTRY:

Why did the pastry shrink away from the sides of the tart pan during baking?

- Pastry was stretched when rolled out

- Pastry was not allowed to rest before and after rolling which made it lose its elasticity before baking

Why did the pasty get hard and tough?

- Pastry was over-mixed in the bowl or kneaded too much
- Too much liquid was added to the flour and butter mixture
- Too much flour was used to dust the work surface for rolling out

Why was the bottom of the tart soggy?

- Cooked pastry shell was not brushed with beaten egg white while still hot
- The cooled pastry case was not brushed with a thin layer of apricot glaze before adding the filling

Why did the pastry collapse as soon as it was removed from the oven?

- Pastry was not baked long enough
- A hole was not pierced through the bottom of the cooked pastry which trapped steam and caused the pastry to soften
- Oven temperature was too high

MERINGUES:

Why did the egg whites take so long to whisk?

- Egg whites were too cold; they must be at room temperature before whisking
- Bowl or whisk was slightly greasy; both must be spotlessly clean
- Eggs were not fresh
- A little yolk was dropped into the whites while separating

Times and Temperatures

- Whites were not lifted high during the whisking to form a good airy structure

Why did a clear syrup run out of the meringues during baking?

- Granulated sugar was used that did not dissolve fully; try using superfine sugar
- Sugar was added too quickly or too much at once
- Some form of excess moisture was in the oven during baking
- The meringue was not baked immediately

Why were the meringues still damp in the middle after baking?

- They were not baked and allowed to dry out in the oven long enough

CREAMS, ICINGS AND FILLINGS:

Why was it difficult to whip the cream into peaks?

- The cream, whisk and bowl were not chilled enough before use
- Cream was not fresh
- Sugar was added too soon in the whipping process

Why does the icing or whipped cream have lumps of confectioners' sugar in it?

- Confectioners' sugar was not sifted before being added; these lumps never disperse once added to the other ingredients

OVEN CHART:

Very slow oven	250 to 275 degrees
Slow oven	300 to 325 degrees
Moderate oven	350 to 375 degrees
Hot oven	400 to 425 degrees
Very hot oven	450 to 475 degrees
Extremely hot oven	500 to 525 degrees

CANDY AND FROSTING (temperature of syrup):

Thread	230 to 234 degrees
Soft ball	234 to 240 degrees
Firm ball	244 to 248 degrees
Hard ball	250 to 266 degrees
Soft crack	270 to 290 degrees
Hard crack	300 to 310 degrees

Contributor's List

The St. Andrew's By-the-Sea Cookbook Committee of *The Outer Banks Companion* wish to express their deep appreciation to the following parishioners and friends of St. Andrew's Church who so generously contributed many of their favorite time-tested recipes. Due to cost factors and similarity of recipes, we were unable to publish all recipes received. We hope that our friends will understand this compromise and share in our enthusiasm for the finished product of *The Outer Banks Companion*.

Elizabeth Anderson
ANONYMOUS
Lisa Armstrong
Shirley Barrett
Ashby Baum
Carolyn Baum
Larry Beemer
Phyllis H.Benoit
Jane Berry
Judy Boatwright
Mary Bobbitt
Edna Bowe
Lois Bradshaw
Jeannie Brake
Carol Brassington
David Brassington
Phyllis Bruce
Margaret R. Burch
Bob Burrell
Kelly Burton
B. J. Butler
Katherine Campbell
Laura Perkins Catoe
Helen Cliborne
Marcia Cline
Emma N. Cooper
Isabel Cooper
Alpha Newsome Copeland
Tammy Cross
Velma J. Crumpler
Faye Lewark Daniels

Elizabeth Davenport
Grant Davenport
William Grant Davenport
Jan DeBlieu
Louise Dollard
Lee Doran
Sarah Spink Downing
Renee Draper
Evelyn Dubose
Anne Embrey
Mary English
Randi Davis Eure
Vera Evans
Debbie Farrell
Pat Fearing
Lib Fearing
Louise Fields
Vanessa Foreman
Melinda Gaines
Dee Garrett
Liz Geidel
Barbara Gibbs
Rev. Charles E. B. Gill
Gia Gonder
Jim Graham
Mary Virginia Jeter Graziani
Donna Keel Greenlee
Bloma Hale
Margaret Harvey
Mike Hayman
Madge F. Hazelwood

Ginny Heinrich
Chelsea Heslin
Cecelia Anne Hill
Barbara Hirsch
Gail Chappell Hodges
Marylou Hogan
Myda Hope
Jean and Don Huston
Margaret Hunt
Theresa "Terrie" Hunter
Mimi and Jim Iacone
Windsor Jacques
Jackie Jenkins
Jean Johnson
Patty Johnson
Rick Kerber
Ruth Lanyon
Myrtha Newsome Lassiter
Julie Layfield
Tish Leonard
Carey LeSieur
Love McCotter Little
Lydia Malco
Tinka Martin
Jean Marx
Lori Marz
Pam Matthews
Nancy Maturo
Frank Maturo
Scott McCaulley
Emma Jane D. McDermott
Connie Mebane
Betty Medlock
Eleanor T. Meekins
Bobbie Murray
Pam Nance
Kathy Nolin

Bruce Nolin
Marilyn O'Bleness
Eunice Goodwin Overman
Lou Overman
Peggy D. Owens
Jeanne Pace
Devin Parsons
Stephanie Nolin Patterson
Mary Peckens
Gigi Phillips
Joyce Pickrel
Jeanne Pool
Patsy Respess
Debbie Runnells
Betty Atwood Ryan
Anna Sadler
Bob Sanders
Karen Sawin
Linda Sharp
Ronald L. Speer
Elizabeth Spencer
St. Andrews by-the-Sea Preschool
Betsy Steketee
Lauren Straub
Gayle Summa
Jo Utley
Bob Vinson
JoKitt Vinson
Mike Walker
Cammie Walker
Richard Welch
Stan White
Linda White
Molly H. Wiggers
Allen W. Wood
Harriet Workman

Index

Index

Index

Index

Index

Index

Index

Index

Index

Index

COMPANION

St. Andrew's By-the-Sea Episcopal Church
P.O. Box 445
Nags Head, NC 27959

Please send _____ copy(ies)   @ $25.00 each _____

Postage and handling   @ $ 3.50 each _____

North Carolina residents add sales tax   @ $ 1.50 each _____

                                                Total _____

Name _____

Address_____

City_____ State _____ Zip_____

*Make checks payable to **St. Andrew's By-the-Sea** — **The Outer Banks Companion***

- -

COMPANION

St. Andrew's By-the-Sea Episcopal Church
P.O. Box 445
Nags Head, NC 27959

Please send _____ copy(ies)   @ $25.00 each _____

Postage and handling   @ $ 3.50 each _____

North Carolina residents add sales tax   @ $ 1.50 each _____

                                                Total _____

Name _____

Address_____

City_____ State _____ Zip_____

*Make checks payable to **St. Andrew's By-the-Sea** — **The Outer Banks Companion***